Theological Dialogs
For The
21st Century

Glenn Rogers

ISBN 978-1-7367041-0-3

Simpson & Brook, Publishers
Abilene, Texas

All of Dr. Rogers' books are available
from Amazon
Search Amazon for *books by Glenn Rogers*

Outline

Introduction

Conclusion

Introduction

Using dialogs to introduce and teach challenging subject matter has been going on since Plato began publishing his philosophical dialogs in ancient Greece. And while dialogs are not typically used to teach theology, it occurred to me as I was writing *Philosophical Dialogs For The 21st Century* that the same approach I used in that book might work in a book about contemporary theological concerns.

My goal in this small book is not to go deeply into complicated theological or biblical questions that scholars enjoy dealing with, but to ask and answer some important but basic questions that many people wonder about, especially people who have not had much in the way of religious or biblical training. You can see this by looking at the outline above.

It is my hope that readers will give serious considerations to the arguments I make through my character, Dr. Kyle Baker, retired professor of philosophy and former missionary and minister. I do not imagine for a moment that everyone who reads this book will agree with every argument Dr. Baker makes, or appreciate the topics raised by the young people who come to him. I'm not necessarily looking for agreement. I'm hoping for an open-mindedness on the part of readers and a willingness to deepen their understanding. If that happens, the time and effort it took to prepare this material will have been worth it.

Why did I choose the specific topics I chose? First, because I believe they are important questions that many people wonder about. Important questions deserve to be answered. Second, because some of them are concerns that are not only religious in nature but also important social concerns that need to be addressed from a religious perspective. Third, my hope is that if non-religious or even anti-religious people read this small book, I might be able to help them understand why people of faith are the way we are. It is clear from the comments you hear from non-religious people that they have no clue as to why we believe what we believe, and why we feel so strongly about it. The only way they can understand it is to chalk it up to religious fanaticism—which is usually associated with uneducated, uninformed people who may not be emotionally stable. I assure you, while some religious people are in fact uneducated and uninformed, most of us are not. Some of us have quite a good bit of education and are at the leading edge of sociocultural and sociopolitical scholarship. Most people of faith are not people of faith because of ignorance or emotional problems, but because of a great deal of study, introspection, and experience—which has led us into the deep faith and commitment that makes us who we are. I hope that in reading these dialogs some of that comes through, and readers will gain insight into the heart and mind of a person of faith.

Chapter 1
Jenna and the Origin of the Bible

"Okay," Jenna said, "Well, my question is, how do you know that the Bible isn't just another ancient book like the Code of Hammurabi or one of those other ancient books?"

My young friend, Conner, had brought Jenna in to talk with me, explaining to her that I knew about stuff like the Bible and philosophy, and that I could answer her question. He brings in a couple of people a week.

Jenna looked to be in her early twenties, like most of Conner's friends, was a pretty, petite young lady, who, so far, seemed above average in her ability to think and communicate. We were sitting in The Roasted Bean, a coffee shop in Abilene, Texas, at a table against the back wall that I had come to think of as *my table* since I have coffee and a scone here every morning around ten and enjoy sitting at this particular table.

"Good question," I said. "If it's just an old book it might have some historical value as it concerns ancient culture; but there are thousands of those around. However, if the Bible, as it claims to be, is of divine origin, then it is likely a book to which human beings ought to pay a great deal of attention."

"You talk like a professor," Jenna said.

"Guilty as charged," I said. "Retired professor of philosophy and cultural studies, former missionary and minister."

"Is that normal?" she asked. "A minister and missionary becoming a philosophy professor?"

"I've never met a philosopher who used to be a minister or a missionary. There may be some out there, but I've never met any of them. I suspect we are something of a unique breed."

"Hmm. Interesting. So what do you do now that you are retired?"

"I work for a think tank called the Marsden Group."

"I've never heard of that. What is it?"

"It a group of conservative scholars who write books and articles, and speak, when invited, at colleges, universities, and other organizations interested in conservative ideas and values."

"Wow. So you are an actual *bone fide* scholar."

I shrugged modestly and said. "That and three bucks will buy me a cup of coffee. What about you? What's your story?"

"My grandpa was a minister," Jenna said. "My dad was a Christian when he was young, but as he got older, he walked away from religion. Said it was irrelevant. Didn't offer him anything that was helpful. Mostly just ritual and people arguing over doctrinal stuff all the time, he said. So he walked away from it. Broke my grandpa's heart. Family gatherings never felt quite right. Anyway, as my grandpa was dying—literally just minutes before he passed—he begged my dad to come back to God. It was really sad. Haunting. I can't get the scene out of my head. And I'm wondering if my grandfather might have been right about the whole religion thing, the Bible, Christ, the church, and all that. He was a very smart man. Wrote some books. I read a couple of them. They had some good stuff in them. But other than that, I have no religious training of any kind, and I don't know where to start. And what I read in his books didn't have anything to do with the kind of questions I have. So, as Conner and I were talking about it, he said you'd be able to answer my questions."

"He did, huh?"

Conner smiled. "Of course I did," he said. "You've been able to answer every question my friends have put to you."

"They just happened to have asked questions I have spent lots of time thinking about."

"Their good fortune," Conner said. "But before we get too deep into this one ..." he was looking at Jenna ... "how about some coffee?"

"I could do with a cup," Jenna said.

While Conner went to get coffee for himself and Jenna, I said, "So, what did your grandfather write?"

"One of the books was about the parables of Jesus; the other one was a devotional book based on some of the psalms."

"Interesting subjects," I said. "But your question is whether or not the Bible is of divine or human origin."

9

"Yes," Jenna said.

"Okay, well, let's see what we can do. The first thing that is important to consider is the age of the Bible. It is an ancient book that has been around for a long time. The oldest parts of it are probably four thousand years old. Maybe older."

"But aren't there lots of really old books?" Jenna asked.

"Sure. But none of them are like the Bible."

"How are they different?"

"Most of the ancient texts are just old books from different cultures. Many are religious texts. Some are law texts, some are business records; some are classified as literature. You mentioned the Code of Hammurabi."

"What are some of the others?"

"There's the Gilgamesh Epic, the Book of the Dead, the Pyramid Texts, just to name a few."

"So if there are other ancient books, why is the Bible thought to be special?" Jenna asked.

"Because the Bible is quite different from other ancient texts."

"How?"

Conner returned with two coffees. Jenna took the lid off her cup and took a sip.

"Well," I said, "for one, the Bible was written over a period of about two thousand years by forty different men from vastly different times and places. Yet there is a unity of focus, a single storyline that underlies the text from beginning to end: something those forty men could not have accomplished without divine assistance."

"What about the Quran?"

10

"Well, first the Quran is not nearly as old as the Bible. It was written in the seventh century AD. Only fourteen hundred years ago. Second, the scope of the Quran is not even remotely like the scope of the Bible. Third, it doesn't tell the kind of story the Bible tells. It's just not the same kind of a book. All you have to do to see that is to read it. And while there may be some similarities between the two books, those similarities can be attributed to Mohammed's familiarity with the Hebrew and Christian scriptures and his desire to claim that he, rather than Jesus, is the great prophet of God—something that would elevate Arab-origin peoples above the Jews—the cultural rivals of the Arab peoples."

"So you're saying there was some sort of ethnic competition between the Jews and the Arabs · in the production of the Quran?"

"Yes."

"So you don't believe the Quran is a holy book in the same way the Bible is a holy book."

"I do not."

"But lots of people do."

"That's right. And I think each person has to read each book and decide which one he or she wants to follow."

"The Bible is an awfully big book."

"It is. I would suggest that one begin by reading the New Testament. It's a lot smaller and tells the most important part of the biblical story. The Gospel of John might be a good place to begin."

"And if I read them both, what will I find?"

"Two very different kinds of books that have a very different feel to them and tell a very different story."

"And you think the one told in the Bible is a better story."

"I do."

"But it is still just a story."

"Being a story doesn't mean it's not true. If someone asked you to tell them the story of your life and you did, would it be the case that the story you told them was not true?"

"No. It would be boring, but I would tell them the truth."

"So there are stories that are true and stories that are not true. I believe the story told in the Bible is true."

"Why?"

"That's the question we're trying to answer, isn't it? And the first reason is the one I've already offered: the age of the Bible, the diversity of authorship, and the unity of message. The second reason is its impact on the world."

"You mean like the number of people who are Christians?"

"That, certainly. Christianity is by far the largest religion in the world. As of 2015, there were 2.3 billion Christians in the world. With a world population of 7.3 billion, that's about thirty-one percent."

"What about the Muslims?"

"There are about 1.8 billion Muslims."

"So a lot more Christians than Muslims."

"Yes. But when we refer to the impact of Christianity in the world, we are not only talking about how many people are Christians, but the impact of the Judeo-Christian perspective on reality and life in so many cultures of the world."

"In what way?" Jenna asked.

"Even in societies where there isn't a formal or official religion, like the United States for instance, the Judeo-Christian perspective and tradition has shaped legal and court systems and moral thinking more than any other single religion or philosophy in the world. The Western legal system, for example, comes pretty much right out of the Old Testament."

"I didn't know that."

"Most of the people in America embrace a moral system that is rooted in a Judeo-Christian perspective even though they may not embrace either Judaism or Christianity as a religion."

"Why is that?"

"Because Christianity developed out of Judaism and became the official religion of the Roman Empire. And when the Roman Empire fell, Christianity is what held Western society together. During the Middle Ages a new social structure evolved that was still deeply rooted in Christian beliefs and perspectives. When people began immigrating to America, they brought their ideas about social structure and religion with them. So, although America was not officially a Christian nation, it was deeply rooted in Christian beliefs."

"And you're saying that no other religion or philosophy can claim to have influenced the number of people and societies as Christianity."

"That's right."

"Hmm. Interesting." She took a sip of her coffee and said, "I hope there's more, though."

"There is," I said. "The message in the Bible is absolutely unique. There is nothing else in any ancient book that comes even close. Or in modern books for that matter. The Bible is in a class by itself."

"So, what, exactly, is the message if the Bible?"

"The message is that the universe, the planet earth, and human beings exist because God created them. Humans are created in God's image, which means that they are essentially the same kind of being he is. In this stage of our existence, we are embodied beings, that is, we exist in relation to our physical body. God is not embodied. He is a mental being that permeates all of reality, material and immaterial. But that difference aside, each human is the same kind of being God is—a thinking, mental being. Metaphorically, we are his offspring. He created us. He loves us, and wants to enjoy a relationship with us. But because we are baby minds, we do not understand how to live well. So, like babies and little kids, we make a mess of things. But God loves us and wants a relationship with us anyway. So he forgives us when we make a mess of things, and hopes that we will want to enjoy a relationship with him. And despite some of the stories in the Old Testament, stories that are rooted in the beliefs and assumptions of the people of the ancient Middle East, he is a God of love and mercy and forgiveness if we are interested in a relationship with him."

"And no other ancient book has a message like that," Jenna said.

"None."

"Okay, so it is a unique story. But how do we know that it is not just something some really creative guys came up with?"

"Fair question. And the answer is fulfilled prophecy."

"Prophecy," she said.

"Prophecy."

"Lots of books have prophecies in them," she said.

"Not like the prophecies in the Bible."

"How are biblical prophecies different?"

"They are extremely specific. And there are dozens and dozens of them."

"Like what?"

"Well, there are over forty prophecies in the Old Testament concerning the coming of the Messiah: Jesus. They tell of things like the incarnation, the birth of Jesus, how he would suffer, how he would be rejected by the people of Israel, the kind of death he would die, his resurrection, all sorts of things that included a lot of very specific details. And that's what makes biblical prophecy different from all other forms of prophecy. Most of what are sometimes called prophecies are very broad and general, like a horoscope or a fortune cookie fortune—you know the kind of thing I mean: *be generous and good things will happen to you*. Biblical prophecy, especially the ones about Jesus, are very specific: when and where he would be born, how he would be tortured and killed. Things like that. And they were foretold hundreds of years in advance."

"So, that means what?"

"Well, since human beings do not know the future and cannot control cosmic events, the only explanation for the source of all those prophecies is God. God gave the men writing the Bible the information about the coming Messiah, or Christ. The writers of scripture were able to prophesy correctly about Jesus because they received divine guidance. God guided them in what they wrote."

"So, you're saying that because there are prophecies about Jesus that appear to have come true, we should accept the Bible as something that God produced."

"Not exactly," I said. "The Bible doesn't claim to be something God produced and dropped into human culture. The Bible claims to be the work of human authors who were guided by God in the composition of the message."

"Can you say that another way?"

"Sure. The Bible claims that God was helping the biblical authors communicate a message that, though it includes a good deal of human cultural beliefs, was ultimately a divine message, a message from God to his human offspring."

"Explain about the human cultural beliefs," Jenna said.

"God did not dictate to the writers the words they were to write. The human authors were not mindless automatons just writing what they were told to write. They were an active part of the process, writing as participants in a given human culture. Their ancient beliefs can be seen in the works they produced. But mixed in with the beliefs of their ancient cultures was the message that God wanted delivered to the people."

"So, when you read the Bible, you have to separate out the ancient culture from the message of God?"

"Yes."

"Isn't that kind of hard to do? How would you know which is which?"

"Yes," I said. "It's hard to do. But it is doable. Admittedly, it involves an ongoing dialog among scholars as to what is human culture and what is divine message, but the message comes through intact. The message God wanted his human children to have is available to them in the Bible."

Jenna leaned back in her chair, thought for a moment, sipped her coffee, and said, "Okay, so, I get what you're saying, but all of what you said doesn't add up to actual proof that the Bible is … I'm not sure … what's the word?"

"Inspired."

"Right," she said. "Inspired."

"You're right. It doesn't. Doesn't absolutely prove anything. But I think it comes close. There is, though, an element of faith."

"So you can never be sure."

"That depends on how you understand faith," I said.

"Isn't faith just something you believe?"

"Some people would say so, but in this case I wouldn't agree with them. I've given you several good reasons, rationally sound arguments I would say, that the Bible is more than just an old book. There are things that are true of the Bible that simply cannot be explained apart from God's involvement in its production. So even though there is an element of faith in accepting the Bible as a divinely inspired book, it is an informed faith that is rooted in rationality. There are good reasons to accept the Bible as divinely inspired."

Jenna thought for a moment. "Okay," she said finally, "Say I accept your premise and I accept that the Bible is of divine origin. Then what?"

"Then you begin studying it."

"It's a big book."

"Yes, it is. And the mistake many people make is to pick it up and begin reading in Genesis One as if it were a contemporary book written for a contemporary audience."

"So, if you don't just pick it up and begin reading it, what do you do?"

"Excellent question. Confusion about how to read the Bible is what causes lots of people to give up on it and walk away. You see, because the Bible is an ancient book written in cultures very different from our own, where the people had completely different worldviews that included dozens of beliefs that were completely unwarranted by today's standards—they were, in fact, very childlike in many of their beliefs—modern readers must read the Bible, especially the Old Testament, very carefully, asking whether what they are reading in any given section is part of the message God wanted to communicate or if it is simply an ancient cultural belief or practice that the human writers included along with God's message."

"To me, that sounds like a nearly impossible task. Do you think the average person is equipped to do that?"

"Probably not. At least not without help."

"Is there any help available?"

"Sure. There are books you can buy and courses you can take."

"So, if I want to read and understand the Bible, I have to buy and read other books?"

"There are some sections of the Bible that just about anyone can read and understand. They are simple, straightforward passages that can be understood and applied by the average person in just about any context. But then there are other passages that require some knowledge of ancient culture and specific communication contexts to understand and apply them correctly."

"Are you saying the average person can't really read and understand the Bible?"

"No. I believe the average person can read and understand the Bible. But some texts in the Bible require some advanced interpretive skills and knowledge to understand, interpret, and apply the message correctly."

"Okay," Jenna said. "I understand what you are saying, but I'm not sure I fully agree yet."

"Fully agree?"

"I understand your arguments, and they are convincing … at least for me. Maybe I wanted to believe in the inspiration of the Bible and just needed a little help to get there. And you've given me that. Sort of."

"Sort of?"

She sipped her coffee and thought for a moment. "I understand what you are saying, but emotionally, I'm not sure I can make a commitment to jumping into the deep end of the pool. Does that make sense?"

"It makes perfectly good sense," I said.

"I agree," Conner said. "Sometimes your brain works faster than your heart, and your heart needs time to catch up."

Jenna considered him for a moment and smiled. Then, to me she said, "So what can I do to help my heart catch up to my brain?"

"Praying is always a good idea. Ask God to help you have the faith and insight and wisdom you need."

"You can ask God to help you have the faith you need?"

"God loves you," I said. "There isn't anything you can't talk with him about."

"That seems odd to me," Jenna said.

"There's a story in the Bible," I said, "in the Gospel of Mark, chapter nine, where a father brings his sick son to Jesus' disciples to be healed. Jesus wasn't there, and the disciples couldn't help the young man. When Jesus arrived, he asked what was going on. The young man's father explained. Jesus was not happy with his disciples' inability to help the young man, but focused his immediate attention on the father and his son. The father said to Jesus, '*if you can do anything, please help.*' Jesus replied '*If I can do anything… to those who believe, everything is possible.*' The boy's father said, '*I do believe. Help my unbelief,*' which is another way of saying, *I have some faith, help me to have more.*"

"And did Jesus give the man more faith?"

"Turns out that what he had was enough. Jesus accepted the faith the man had and healed his son."

"So your point is that if I sort of believe that the Bible is the word of God, if I ask God to help me work through my questions and doubts, he will, and I will be able to accept the Bible as God's communication to his human children."

"Perhaps," I said. "God knows what you really believe, what you really think, and what you really want. He answers prayer based on what he knows to be the case, and what he knows will happen if he does this or that. Prayer isn't a Christmas wish list, and God isn't Santa Claus."

"That sounds like a cop-out. Maybe God will answer your prayer, maybe he won't. How do you ever know if he has or not? Maybe what happens is simply happenstance or coincidence."

"That's a good question. And the answer is that if you enjoy an intimate relationship with God, talking to and interacting with him on a regular basis, you know he's responding to you, and you know you can trust his reply."

"That seems awfully subjective," Jenna said.

"All relationships are subjective," I said. "They are about the interactions of the people involved in the relationship. What else would they be but subjective?"

She sipped her coffee, thought about it, and said, "I guess that's so."

I could see she was thinking, so I sat quietly.

"Ok," she said after a moment. "I get what you are saying about the Bible being different from all other books, ancient or modern. I get that, and the thing about fulfilled prophecy is a convincing argument. But if the Bible is God's communication to human beings, why is there so much in it that seems so out of place?"

"Ahh, that's really the issue, isn't it?"

"What do you mean?"

"The main reason, I think, that people question the origin of the Bible is because there's stuff in it they don't like. They don't understand how to read it or study it, they don't understand how to interpret it, and when they read something they don't understand or disagree with, the simplest way around it is to say it is just the opinions of a bunch of old dead Jewish guys, so who cares what they thought."

"You really think that's the problem?"

"I do."

"So, what's the solution?"

"People need to learn how to read, study, and interpret the Scriptures. They need to read some books that explain how to do those things. They need to understand the difference between the Old Testament and the New. They need to understand the historical context of the Scriptures, the culture of people to whom the different parts of the Bible were written, the different kinds of language used; they need to understand that you can't pick up an ancient cross-cultural text and read it as if it were a contemporary book. Studying and understanding the Bible is a complex process."

"Sounds like a lot of work."

"It is. But it's worth it."

Jenna thought for a moment. She began to nod to herself. "I see what you're saying. But this is not a simple thing. I need time to think."

"And you need to continue to read the Bible, especially the New Testament, and to ask God to help you understand."

"Yeah," she said. "I think you are right. But I'd also like to come back and talk to you some more after I do that. Would that be possible?"

"Absolutely."

As Conner and Jenna left, I said a silent prayer, thanking God for Conner, and asking God to help Jenna in her journey toward faith.

Chapter 2
Randal and How to Understand
and Interpret the Bible

"Hi, Dr. Baker," Conner said as he and another young man arrived at my table. "This is Randal, a friend of mine."

"Randal," I said, as I stood to shake his hand. He had reddish-orange hair, freckles, fair skin, and blue eyes. I suspected Irish heritage. "Nice to meet you," I said and gestured to the chairs. "Have a seat."

"I'll go get us some coffee," Conner said.

"And a scone," Randal said. "Get me a scone. I'll pay you back."

"Uh-huh," Conner said smiling. "When have you ever paid me back?"

"Yeah, but this time I will," Randal said. "I got a job, remember?"

"You want anything, Dr. Baker?" Conner asked.

"I'm good. Thanks."

Conner went to get the coffee and scones, and I asked Randal how he knew Conner.

"We've known each other since junior high school. Girl I'm dating got me interested in Christianity, and I mentioned it to Conner. We got to talking about the Bible, and he told me about the conversation he had with you about his brother's death. That discussion led us into several discussions about how to interpret the Bible, and he said I should talk to you about it."

"Be glad to," I said as Conner returned with two coffees and two scones.

"Glad to what?" Conner said as he put a coffee and scone down in front of Randal.

"Talk to Randal about biblical hermeneutics."

"Biblical what?" Randal asked.

"Hermeneutics," I said. "The study of interpretation."

"So, there's an entire field of study that has to do with how to interpret the Bible?"

"Not just the Bible," I said, "but literature in general. But biblical hermeneutics is a very important theological concern."

"Is this going to be complicated and technical?" Randal asked.

"Doesn't have to be," I said. "I think we can keep it simple enough."

"Good. Because I hadn't anticipated having to think very hard about this."

I smiled.

Randal sipped his coffee, took a bite of his scone, and said, "Where do we begin our discussion of ... what was it, hermeneutics?"

"Yes, hermeneutics. And I think the most important point to make right up front is when it comes to reading and interpreting the Bible, we must remember that the Bible is an ancient cross-cultural text that was written to specific peoples in different historical and cultural contexts. And because that is the case, it is absolutely inappropriate to simply pick it up and begin reading at some point in the text and apply it as if it were written by a contemporary Western author to a contemporary Western audience."

"I'm not sure I understand what that means."

"Do you have a Bible app on your phone?"

"Yes."

"Look up Jeremiah 29:11."

Randal opened his app and found the verse.

"Read it out loud."

"'For I know the plans I have for you,' declares the Lord, 'plans to prosper you and not to harm you, plans to give you hope for the future.'"

"Good," I said. "What does that seem to be saying?"

"That the Lord has good things in store for his people." Randal said. "That good stuff not bad stuff is going to happen to them."

"Yes. I think that's what most people would get from that verse. But now go back and read the first fourteen verses of the chapter."

Randal scrolled back up to the beginning of the chapter and began reading. *"This is the text of the letter that the prophet Jeremiah sent from Jerusalem to the surviving elders among the exiles and to the priests, and the prophets and all the other people Nebuchadnezzar had carried into exile from Jerusalem to Babylon. (This was after King*

Jehoiachin and the queen mother, and the court officials and the leaders of Judah and Jerusalem, the craftsmen and the artisans had gone into exile from Jerusalem.) He entrusted the letter to Elasah son of Shaphan and to Gemariah son of Hilkiah, whom Zedekiah king of Judah sent to King Nebuchadnezzar in Babylon. It said:

This is what the Lord Almighty, the God of Israel says to all I carried into exile from Jerusalem to Babylon: 'Build houses and settle down; plant gardens and eat what they produce. Marry and have sons and daughters; find wives for your sons and give your daughters in marriage, so that they too may have sons and daughters. Increase in number there; do not decrease. Also, seek the peace and prosperity of the city to which I have carried you into exile. Pray to the Lord for it, because if it prospers, you too will prosper.' Yes, this is what the Lord Almighty, the God of Israel says, 'Do not let the prophets and diviners among you deceive you. Do not listen to the dreams you encourage them to have. They are prophesying lies to you in my name. I have not sent them,' declares the Lord.

This is what the Lord says: 'When seventy years are completed for Babylon, I will come to you and fulfill my gracious promise to bring you back to this place. For I know the plans I have for you,' declares the Lord, 'plans to prosper you and not harm you, plans to give you hope and a future. Then you will call on me and come to me and find me when you seek me with all your heart. I will be found by you,' declares the Lord, 'and will bring you back from captivity. I will gather you from all the nations and places where I have banished you,' declares the Lord, "and will bring you back to the place from which I carried you into exile.'"

"Very good," I said. "So having read verse eleven in the context of the first fourteen verses, what is it talking about?"

"It's talking about the people of Israel who have been exiled from Palestine and who, after seventy years will be brought back and blessed."

I nodded. "Exactly. So what makes anyone think that verse eleven can be lifted out of its historical context and applied to people who are not the people of Israel living in exile?"

"I don't know," Randal said.

"What they usually say is that they understand the historical context, but that the verse can be used in a secondary application manner so that it applies to all people who seek the Lord."

Randall thought about that for a minute. Finally, he said, "Can it?"

"Why would you think it can be?"

"I don't know. That's why I'm asking."

"Did your parents ever say anything to you that applied only to you?"

"What do you mean? Like that they loved me or something?"

"Sure. Or maybe something more specific, like, *When we die we are leaving you this house and the house out at the lake.*"

"Not that exact thing, but something like it. Sure."

"Okay. So what if someone was listening in on that conversation, a friend of yours named Bill, and later Bill

27

mentioned to you that he was really looking forward to inheriting the lake house? How would you react?"

"I guess I would tell Bill that my parents were talking to me, not to him. He wasn't going to be inheriting the lake house."

"Exactly. And you'd be right. When a promise is made to a specific person or group of people, other people cannot come along and lay claim to those promises."

"So, does that mean that there is no secondary application in the Bible?"

"No, doesn't mean that. There are texts that have secondary applications. But because there are some texts that have secondary applications does not mean that you can create a secondary application to whatever text you want."

"Can you give me an example?"

"Sure. Consider Psalm 22. Most scholars understand Psalm 22 to be a psalm of David that applies first to David. In the psalm he's crying out about the unjust suffering he's having to endure. But the psalm is also considered a Messianic psalm, which means it has a secondary application to Jesus."

"Okay," Randal said, "so some passages have a secondary application and some don't."

"Correct," I said.

"And some," Randal said, "that have a secondary application have a specific application, like to Jesus or someone else."

"Yes."

"Are there any that have, I don't know, what, an open-ended secondary application that can be applied to people in general?"

"Some. Yes."

"So, how do you know which are which?"

"That's a good question. And the answer is that it requires a lot of study and prayer, asking God to help you understand, especially when the text under consideration is from the Old Testament because most of what is in the Old Testament has to do specifically with the ancient nation of Israel. So the process is more difficult when dealing with the Old Testament than with the New. But one of the basic rules for every text, Old Testament or New, is that if you are going to apply a text to people in general, there must be something in the context of the passage under consideration that makes it clear that a broader or secondary application would be appropriate."

Randal was nodding.

"For instance," I said, "In John 4, when Jesus visited the town of Cana, an official whose son was sick came to Jesus asking him to heal the boy. Jesus said to the man, '*You may go. Your son will live.*' Based on that text, should every parent who has a sick child assume that Jesus will heal the child?"

"Probably not," Randal said.

"Why not?"

"Because Jesus was talking to a specific man about his son. Unless there's something in the larger context that suggests that Jesus will heal all sick children, there's no reason to believe that he will."

"Correct. Jesus didn't heal all sick people during his earthly ministry, and he doesn't heal all sick people today. So there's no reason to assume that the text in John 4 applies to anyone other than the man and boy in that story. However,

29

in Second Corinthians 5, there's a verse that says, '*if anyone is in Christ, he is a new creation.*' Anyone. Not a specific person, but anyone. Obviously, that applies to anyone. Everyone."

"Okay, I see what you are saying, but I'm still not entirely clear on how that applies to reading, let's say, the book of Romans and applying it to people today."

"Okay, that's a good question. Use your app to go to Romans 12:1-2."

Randal found the passage and read it: "*Therefore, I urge you, brothers, in view of God's mercy, to offer your bodies as living sacrifices, holy and pleasing to God—this is your spiritual act of worship. Do not conform any longer to the pattern of this world, but be transformed by the renewing of your mind. Then you will be able to test and approve what God's will is—his good, pleasing, and perfect will.*"

"Okay," I said, "how is this text different from the text in Jeremiah?"

"That text was written to the Israelites who were in exile. God was promising them that he would bring them back from Babylon to Palestine."

"Yes."

"Okay," Randal said, "but here, the Apostle Paul is writing to the Christians in Rome."

"Yes."

"So if the text in Jeremiah is specific only to the Israelites, why isn't this text specific only to the Christians in Rome?"

"Because what Jeremiah wrote had to do specifically to the Israelites in their time and place—they would live in exile for seventy years and then be allowed to return to

Palestine. Promises made to them regarding that time and place can't be appropriated by people and applied to other times and places. But what Paul wrote to the believers in Rome is not specific to them because of who they were and the circumstances they were in. Paul said the same kinds of things to Christians in other cities throughout the Roman Empire. When you read the letters in the New Testament, it is obvious that the advice given, in most cases, is given to Christians in general and can be applied to Christians in general."

"In most cases," Randal said.

"Yes. There are some things in the New Testament that are specific to individuals or churches in a given set of circumstances. For instance, when Paul's young associate, Timothy, was in Ephesus, they were having problems with some of the women who were teaching in the church there. Apparently, some of the women who had very likely been leaders and teachers in the cult of Diana, the goddess of Ephesus, had been converted to Christianity. Some of them may have considered themselves qualified to teach in the church there in Ephesus. But if they had not been Christians very long, some of the things they taught may have been incorrect and causing problems. Timothy needed some advice about how to handle the problem. To Paul, it seemed that the simplest solution was to not allow women to teach. Rather than allowing some women to teach and others not, Paul's advice to Timothy was simply to not allow any women there in Ephesus to teach. That's what he decided for the church in Ephesus. However, in Corinth, women were allowed to teach as long as they covered their head while doing so."

"Covered their head?"

"In ancient societies where women were required to be submissive to men, women usually covered their heads to show that they understood their secondary place in society. So, in the church in Corinth, as long as a woman wore a head covering she could teach, but in Ephesus women could not teach even if they covered their heads. The reason was because of a specific situation in the city of Ephesus. Over the centuries, failing to understand why Paul gave different advice to different churches on the matter of women teachers has caused a lot of problems in the modern church."

Randal was nodding to himself. "Okay, I think I see. This interpretation thing is not easy."

"No," I said, "it's not. You can't pick up an ancient cross-cultural text and read and understand it as if it were written by a contemporary Western author to a contemporary Western audience. That just doesn't work."

"Okay, so, are there other interpretive concerns?"

"Yes," I said. "A couple more big ones."

"Like what?"

"Like cultural, and symbolic or figurative language."

"You said this wasn't going to be complicated."

I chuckled and paused to drink some of my coffee. "Okay," I said. "Maybe it's a little complicated, but I think you can manage it."

Randal drank some of his coffee and ate some of his scone. "Okay," he said after a minute. "So, culture."

I nodded. "The Bible wasn't written in a cultural vacuum. The culture of the men who wrote the biblical text shaped and impacted them as completely as our culture shapes and impacts us."

"What has their culture got to do with how we interpret the Bible?"

"Culture is everything about how a group of people live. The culture you grow up in teaches you how to think, what to think, how to speak, how to dress, how to work and play, what to eat and how to eat it, how families are structured, how children are raised and educated, what they are taught, how people get married, how they are buried, what you believe about the natural world and the supernatural world, about whether you think of yourself as an individual or part of a collective—your culture impacts every aspect of who you are and how you are."

"Wow. Hadn't really thought about it like that."

"And because culture influences you so thoroughly, even though you have free will, you exercise it within the framework of your cultural context."

"So, you're saying that the guys who wrote the Bible, even though God was guiding them in the writing process, what they wrote was impacted by their culture."

"Exactly. See, this isn't that hard."

"So, when you are interpreting the Bible, you have to factor in the culture of the places where the biblical authors lived."

"Yes."

"So, does that mean that everything in the Bible is just a product of the culture of the guys who wrote it?"

"No, because God was guiding the guys who wrote it. What was written was written from the cultural perspective of the people it was written to—otherwise they wouldn't have been able to understand it. But underlying the culture forms, the spiritual ideas involved transcended the cultural practices of that time and place."

"I'm sorry," Randal said, "but you kind of lost me."

"Okay, think about the Old Testament system of worship: lots of ritual and ceremony, altars, sacrifices, blood, death—ideas and practices that many modern people find repulsive. But those kinds of things were reflective of the way the world was at that time. And the specific practices, sacrificing a lamb, let's say, symbolically represented the sacrifice of Jesus on the cross. Just about everything in the Old Testament system of worship represented an idea that God wanted the people to understand. So he used the common features of the culture of the Middle East—priests, temples, sacrifices—to represent the spiritual truths he wanted them to understand."

"So the stuff that was actually going on was not the point?"

"Not the primary point. The point was the spiritual things, the physical activities represented. This is the case even in the New Testament."

"I need an example," Randal said.

"Okay, take the Lord's Supper or Communion as an example. In the first century when Christianity was established, Christians met for worship each week, each Sunday, and participated in the Lord's Supper, Communion, in which they ate bread and drank wine that represented the body and blood of Jesus. The physical bread and wine are merely symbols that serve to remind us that Jesus sacrificed his body and blood on the cross so we, sinful people, could be forgiven and enjoy an intimate relationship with God.

Eating the bread and drinking the wine is important, but they are only physical symbols that represent a spiritual reality."

"I see," Randal said.

"But why," I asked, "did Jesus use bread and wine as symbols to help us focus on a spiritual reality?"

"No idea," Randal said.

"Because when he established the Lord's Supper, he and his closest followers were participating in another spiritual ritual from the Old Covenant, the Passover, that had been instituted to help the Jews remember that God had freed them from Egyptian slavery. And in that ritual, which was also a meal, they ate unleavened bread and drank wine. So, in the meal Jesus was eating, they had bread and wine. He used the bread and wine of one ritual to establish another ritual, to help Christians focus on his sacrifice on their behalf."

"Okay," Randal said. "I think I see that, but I'm not clear on how that impacts biblical interpretation."

"There are all sorts of things in the Bible, both Old and New Testaments, that were features of different ancient cultures. Some of them are designed to help us understand important spiritual truths, and some of them are simply references to cultural practices of a given time and place. What we have to do is separate them out—which is not easy to do."

"Can you give me an example?"

"Sure. When Paul wrote one of his letters to the church in Corinth, he told them that they should greet each other with a holy kiss—a kiss on the cheek, often on both cheeks. It was a way of showing friendship and connection. It was a culturally appropriate way of greeting people that would work in the Christian community. But the question is, do all Christians in all places throughout all times have to greet each other with a kiss on the cheek? Most biblical scholars do not think so. The important thing is recognizing and greeting fellow Christians as brothers and sisters in the family of God. The particular form of greeting—a kiss on the cheek, bowing, shaking hands—is not important. It has nothing to do with the kind of person one is and how one demonstrates the family aspect of the Christian community. A heartfelt greeting is an expression of love. The form of that greeting is not crucial and can change from one culture to another."

Randal nodded and took another sip of his coffee.

"Another example," I said, "is what Paul said about women not cutting their hair short and men not letting their hair grow long."

"A woman wasn't allowed to have short hair?"

"Not in the first century. Then, the only women who had short hair were women of questionable moral character. Prostitutes. Respectable women let their hair grow long. So Paul said it was shameful for a woman to have short hair. He also said it was unnatural for a man to have long hair."

"That seems really strange," Randal said.

"Sure it does. Because in our culture, the length of one's hair doesn't have anything to do with the kind of person you are, with your moral character. In other words, in our culture the length of a woman's hair hasn't got anything to do with what kind of a woman she is. The length of a man's hair hasn't got anything to do with the kind of man he is. The length of one's hair is a cultural concern, not a moral or spiritual concern."

"Okay," Randal said. "I see that. So, is there some kind of a formula you can use to figure out what is only a cultural feature of a given time and place and doesn't need to be replicated in our culture?"

"I don't think you can call it a formula," I said. "But basically you look at a particular feature or behavior from the ancient world and analyze it to see if it involves something fundamental to human interaction that needs to be replicated for the sake of one's relationship with God and other people, or if it is a behavior that can be replaced with something else that works just as well."

"Like replacing a kiss on the cheek with a handshake."

"Sure. Or like replacing the idea of women being subservient to men with the idea of women being equal with men."

"That has to do with ... what was it called?"

"Patriarchy."

"Yeah. The idea that men were the leaders, and women had to be quiet and follow along behind."

"Yes," I said. "And that's a good example, because many people assume that because patriarchy is present in the Bible, it is there because God invented the idea and wants women to be subservient rather than it being present in the Bible simply because it was part of the culture of that time and place."

"Okay," Randal said. "I think I get it. You also said something about figurative or symbolic language?"

"Yes. The use of language is a highly complex process, as is understanding how it is used and what is meant."

37

"But we use language every day," Randal said. "Even children use it. I'm not sure we normally think about it as being a complex process."

"Have you ever been talking with someone and had to stop and say, *No, that's not what I meant*?

"Sure. Everyone has."

"Why?"

"Why?"

"Yeah, why did that happen?"

"Because the other person misunderstood what I meant."

"Why?"

"Because he or she wasn't listening very well."

"Or because you weren't communicating very well."

"I'm pretty sure that wasn't it," Randal said and smiled.

I returned his smile. "Or, because the other person understood the words you used differently than you did."

"We were both speaking English, so ..."

"Yes, but words can have more than one meaning or be understood differently by different people, even if they are speaking the same language."

"Okay, so that's why you say it's a complex process."

"Yes. And to complicate things further, sometimes we say things that we do not intend for anyone to take literally."

"Like referring to one of the cheerleaders at school," Randal said, "as a Twinkie."

"Not a nice thing to do, but, yes. Or saying that someone is dumber than a bag of rocks. Or saying it is as hot as blazes outside. Or using metaphors like, *he was a nervous as a long-tailed cat in a room full of rocking chairs*. Understanding the use of figurative language is a learned skill, and understanding them in a language that is not your primary or first language is especially challenging."

"And the Bible has figurative language in it?"

"Lot's of it. In the Old and New Testaments."

"Like what?"

"Well, consider the metaphors used to help us understand God. The Bible speaks of God as a father, a husband, a shepherd, a king, a judge, a strong and mighty tower or fortress, and many others. But he isn't literally any of those things. He's an eternally existing mind."

"So why describe him in those other ways?"

"To help people understand him, how he deals with human beings, what a relationship with him is like."

"I'm not sure I'm getting what you mean."

"Okay, the people of the ancient world were not highly educated and had a number of beliefs that got in the way of their understanding of God. So to help them understand him better, who and what he was, and how being in a relationship with him worked, he revealed himself to the biblical authors in metaphorical ways. If he had said to them, I am the eternally existing mind, they would have said, *What?* So instead, he said, You are sheep, and I'm your shepherd. You are my children, and I'm your father. You are my subjects, and I'm your king. Even with those simple illustrations, they still had difficulty understanding who and what he was, but those metaphors made it a little easier. The problem is that many people today take those metaphors literally.

"In what way?"

"When I was working on my Ph.D.," I said, "I was in a seminar on communication theory. We each had to write a fifty-page paper on some aspect of communication, and I chose to write on biblical metaphors. So I went through the Old and New Testament and looked at all the metaphors used. My point was to explain that the metaphors were figurative language used in an analogous manner and not to be understood literally. We had to make a copy of the paper for each student, and we all had to read and comment on each other's papers. In the class session where we commented on each other's papers, one of the other doctoral candidates explained to me, very patiently so I would understand, that while it is true that God is not literally a shepherd or a father and other such things, he was literally our king. There didn't seem to be any point in arguing with him, so I just smiled and let the comment pass. Obviously, he missed the point I was making in my paper. You'd be surprised at how many people understand the figurative language in the Bible in a literal way."

"Which means that they misunderstand what they are reading," Randal said.

"Yes."

"Okay, so, if I understand what you are telling me, when I read the Bible, I need to be mindful of the cultural concerns and of the Bible's use of figurative language."

"Yes," I said. "And you need to remember that picking up an ancient cross-cultural text and utilizing simple literalism as a method of interpretation is foolish."

"Simple literalism."

"Yeah. It's the idea that you read it, and it says what it means and it means what it says. Just read it and understand it in a literal way."

"You can't understand the Bible in a literally way?"

"Some of it, sure. But not all of it. When Jesus was instituting the Lord's Supper, he said the bread was his body and the wine was his blood. Did he mean that literally? When you put the bread in your mouth, are you literally eating the body of Jesus? Of course not. That's just plain silly. When you drink the wine, are you literally drinking the blood of Jesus? No. The bread and the wine represent his body and his blood. But there are millions and millions of Christians out there who understand Jesus' words literally, which is just silly… and sad." I realized I had gotten ramped up and was no longer my usual calm self. "They believe that when you put the bread into your mouth, it magically transforms and becomes the literal body of Jesus. And the wine magically transforms and literally becomes the blood of Jesus. And that is just one example. The single biggest mistake people make in interpreting the Bible is to understand everything they read in it in a literal way. It causes lots of misunderstandings and silliness."

Conner said, "Wow, Dr. Baker, you don't usually get all worked up like that. This is a big deal to you, isn't it?"

"It is. I deal in truth. And literalism in biblical interpretation often leads to confusion and fails to reveal the truth of Scripture. So, yeah, it really bothers me. Sorry if I got too, as you say, worked up."

"No," Randal said. "You explained and illustrated the whole thing very well. I get what you are saying. The hard part's going to be figuring it all out as I'm studying the Bible."

"Well," I said, "if you need to talk again, I'm here every morning at ten."

Chapter 3
Susan and God's Sovereignty vs.
Human Free Will

I had arrived earlier than normal at the Roasted Bean coffee shop to meet with a young man named Chris who had some questions about baptism as it was practiced by Christians in the first century. It was now just after ten, and as Chris was leaving, Conner came through the front door with a young woman who looked to be in her early twenties. She had short brown hair, and was wearing a snug tee shirt, jeans, and cowboy boots—or since she was wearing them maybe they were they cowgirl boots. I wasn't sure. They went to the counter and got coffee and came back to my table.

"Hi, Dr. Baker," Conner said as they approached my table.

I stood. "Hi, Conner. How's everything?"

"Couldn't be better. This is my friend Susan. Susan, Dr. Baker." Susan had a firm handshake and a voice filled with confidence. I invited them to sit and said that I needed to refill my coffee. When I returned and sat down, I said, "So, what's on the agenda for today, Conner?"

"Susan has some questions about how human free will works with or against God's sovereignty."

"That's a challenging subject," I said. Looking at Susan I said, "Tell me about your concerns."

"Well," she said. "First, how do we know that we have free will? I've heard some people argue that free will is just an illusion. That we are biologically programmed from prehistoric times, and what seems to be free will is just us following our programming. Then others say that God wills everything that we do. That he controls us, and human free will is just an illusion. And then others say that we really are self-determined. So which is it? Is there any way to actually know?"

"That's a good question, and the answer is yes we can know, and yes we really do have free will."

"How do you know?"

"Let's start," I said, "with the idea that God wills and controls all things. This is a Calvinistic idea. God is sovereign, and therefore controls all things. Well, God is sovereign, but that doesn't means he controls all things. A lot of bad stuff happens in the world. Is God responsible for it? Does he cause it to happen? Does he predestine people to be evil and do evil things? Of course, he doesn't. The idea that God predestines people to do or be evil and then punishes them for doing it is ridiculous. In his sovereignty, God chose to give people free will. In fact, because he created humans in his image, they are, by default, self-determined just as God is self-determined. So, that's point number one: the fact that God is sovereign does not require that he controls everything. As the sovereign God, he can decide to make people in his image, which requires that they have free will, because rational, highly aware beings are of necessity self-determined. Being sovereign does not require that God controls all things. Point number two, if God controls all things, then he is the cause of all the evil in the world, which is utterly inconsistent with his nature. God is perfectly good; he does not do evil, neither does he make people do evil. Point number three, if God did control people, causing them to do both good and evil, if they do the evil that he directs them to do, and he then condemns and punishes them as evildoers, he is the most monstrous evil that there can be. You can't make someone do evil and then punish them for doing evil. That's both ugly and silly."

"Hmm," Susan said. "I hadn't thought of it from that point of view."

I smiled, and I sipped my coffee. I also took a bite of the scone I'd decided to buy while getting more coffee.

Susan drank some of her coffee as well as she considered what I had said. Then, "Okay," she said, "I get it that God doesn't control everything. The only way you can make that idea work is if you make God responsible for all the evil in the world. So I agree with you. Silly idea. But what about the idea that we don't really make choices, we're just following ancient biological programming?"

"Well, the problem with that idea—which is called called determinism, or mechanistic determinism—is that there is no evidence of any kind that such a thing is the case. The idea that biological programming determines how we behave is a position arrived at deductively because so many scientists and philosophers have embraced materialism—

which is the idea that people are only physical beings, a body controlled by a brain. Since you are entirely a biological organism, they argue, all you do is carry out biological programming. You do not engage in introspection, weighing alternatives, because you have no alternatives. You just follow your programming. But what evidence suggests anything of that sort? None. In fact, all the evidence regarding self-determination suggests that you do, in fact, have alternatives, and that you engage in introspection in selecting the alternative you prefer."

Susan considered that for a moment and then said, "So it sounds like you are saying that the argument in favor of self-determination is basically personal experience."

"Yes. You know you are self-determined because you know you have alternatives—you can choose between this or that—and you do, in fact, choose one alternative over the other."

"But how do we know there is no ancient programming involved in the choices we make?"

"If there were, how would it work? For instance, it is a little chilly out, so I'm wearing a sport jacket. The one I chose to wear today happens to be corduroy. I could have chosen wool or leather. What sort of ancient programming could have prompted me to select corduroy over leather or wool, especially given that corduroy didn't even exist in ancient times?"

"I couldn't even begin to guess," Susan said.

"If you go into a restaurant," I said, "and order a salad, what kind of ancient programming could prompt you to order ranch dressing for your salad instead of raspberry vinaigrette? Or vice versa?"

"No idea."

"Of course not. No one has any idea. No one to date who advocates mechanistic determinism has been able to offer an explanation of how ancient biological programming could determine why anyone would order ranch dressing instead of raspberry vinaigrette, or why you might to decide on a given day to wear a green blouse instead of a brown one."

"And simply liking the taste of ranch dressing over raspberry vinaigrette would not be a good answer?"

"It's probably a good answer for why you made the choice you made, but how did some kind of ancient programming lead you to that choice? Why do you *like* ranch better than the vinaigrette? How would biological programming account for the subjectivism associated with liking the taste of one thing over another?"

And you've read sufficiently," Susan said, "to know that no one has been able to offer a satisfactory explanation?"

"I have."

She drank some more of her coffee and said, "Okay, then, if God's not in control of everything, and we are not following some kind of ancient biological programming, then we must be self-determined. But if God created us as self-determined beings, yet he is sovereign, how do you reconcile those two things? How can God be sovereign while I am self-determined? I struggle with that."

"I understand. I think the key is simply to understand that the idea of God being sovereign does not require that he control everything."

"And apparently some people think it does?"

"Yes. It is rooted in a simplistic, literalistic way of understanding language. Last week Conner brought another of his friends by, and we talked about the challenges of simplistic literalism as a fundamental approach to biblical interpretation."

"I think I see where you are going," Susan said, "but maybe an example would help."

"Okay, think of the CEO of a large corporation. In fact, think of Bill Gates when he was still running Microsoft. It was his company. He was in charge. But he didn't do everything that needed to be done or that got done. He delegated authority for all kinds of stuff to other people. That's the way all CEOs work. Now, God is not a corporate CEO, and the analogy breaks down if you push it too far. But as a general analogy it works. God created the world and everything and everyone in it. He's God; he's in charge. We can say he is sovereign. But that does not mean or require that he make all the decisions so that he is directly responsible for all that happens. He has created humans as rational, highly aware beings who realize that they have alternatives. They weigh their alternatives and make choices. They have free will. And God, having created humans in his image, knew full well what that would entail. People who have free will sometimes make the wrong choices. Sometimes they do bad things. But they, not God, are the ones who made those choice to do those bad things."

"So people make bad choices," Susan said, "and people get hurt, and there is lots of suffering in the world. Are you suggesting that God simply has to put up with that?"

"Yes."

"Why? God can do anything. Why does he have to put up with what foolish humans do?"

"He has to put up with it because there are some things that even God can't do."

"Like what?"

"He can't make a square triangle, or a round square, or a triangular circle."

"What?"

"What is the definition of a square?"

"A square. I'm sorry. I'm not following you."

Conner spoke up and said, "A square is an object with four sides of equal length."

"Right," I said. "Now, suppose God makes a square and then removes one of the sides. What has he got left?"

"I don't know," Susan said.

"I don't either," I said. "But whatever it is, it is no longer a square. Not even God can remove one of the sides of a square and still have a square left after he does. Because of what a square is, a three-sided square is simply impossible."

"I don't understand what this has got to do with sovereignty and free will."

"If a human is created in God's image and as a result has free will, then not even God can take away a person's free will and still have a person, a human being, left when he's through."

Susan considered me for a long moment and sipped her coffee. "So, you're saying that because God created humans in his image, he has to allow them to do whatever they want."

"Yes."

49

"And if he doesn't, if he overrides their free will, he somehow violates their humanity?"

"Yes. A human being, by virtue of definition, is a being that is self-determined. God can no more take away a human's free will and still have a human left when he's done than he can take away one side of a square and still have a square left when he's done."

"I never thought of it that way before."

I smiled and drank some of my coffee, which was getting cold. I must have grimaced or something, because Conner said, "Want me to warm that up for you?"

"That'd be nice. Thanks."

"So, what you're saying," Susan said, "is that even though God is sovereign, he had made people so they have free will, and when they make bad choices, he just has to put up with it."

"Just like parents have to put up with the bad choices their kids make."

"Okay, so I'm a self-determined person. I make my own decisions. Our minister says that God has a plan for your life. How do you reconcile God having a plan for people's lives and people having free will?"

"That's an excellent question. There's a lot of pop theology floating around out there, and one of the popular ideas right now is that God has a plan for your life. The problem with that idea is that there is no text in the Bible that says that."

"Really."

Conner returned with my coffee. "Thanks, Conner." Then to Susan, I said, "Yes. There are some texts that speak of God's plans for the Israelites or some other specific person, but if you read those texts in context, you see that they apply to a specific person or group of people. And from that, you cannot assume that God, therefore, has a plan for each person's life."

"Can you show me a text where that would be the case?"

"Sure. You got a Bible program on your phone?"

"Sure."

"Look up Jeremiah 29:11"

She read it. "Sounds like it's saying God has plans for his people."

"Sure it does. Now go back up and read from verse one to verse fourteen."

She read it to herself and said, "Ah. I see what you are saying. God was talking to Israel. You're saying that you can't take what he said to them in a specific situation and generalize it and apply it to everyone."

"Correct."

"And you're sure the Bible doesn't talk about God having a plan for each person's life."

"I'm sure. The Bible says God has a plan for how he is going to save people from their sins. It's the same plan for everyone. The Bible explains that God knows who is going to be saved and who's not. But nowhere does it say that God has a *plan* for each person's life, for how his or her life is going to go. That concept is simply incompatible with human self-determination."

"In other words," Susan said, "I can't make my own decisions if God has a plan he's enacting for me."

"Exactly."

"What if my decision is to follow God's will?"

"Then you, using your free will, have decided to follow God's will. That's not the same as him having a plan for your life that he's already got all worked out."

"Okay, I see that. But what about this idea that God knows what I going to do before I do it? If he already knows what I'm going to do, then I can't really do anything different from what he knows is going to happen, can I?"

"Some people have made that argument. You can trace it back to at least the 1800s. I think the fallacy in that reasoning is in not understanding the basis of God's foreknowledge."

"Which is what?" she said, and took a sip of her coffee.

"We exist within and are limited to the time-space continuum. We identify a past, a present, and a future. The past is gone and cannot be changed. The present is here now and we do what we do in the present. The future, for us, does not yet exist, and we do not know what it will be. God, however, as the creator of the universe, which includes the time-space continuum, is not limited to or by the time-space continuum. He existed before he created the time-space continuum, and he exists outside its boundaries. So he is not bound by time. For God, there is no past or future. There is only one continuous or ongoing reality. That which is the future for us is only future for us, not for God. For God, our future is part of the ongoing reality. So he is aware of what is, even when some of it is, for us, still the future."

"Okay, but because he knows the future, can it happen differently than what he knows it to be?"

"Asking the question that way," I said, "is like standing on your head on the floor so you can get a better view of the ceiling. Since we are self-determined beings, we decide what to do, and we do it when we do it. God is aware of our decision and subsequent behavior. Because he knows what we will do in what to us is our future, does not mean that he had anything to do with our decision. And what he knows you or I will do is what we do. His observation of what we do does not limit us. The way you are asking the question suggests that we can do what we do and then somehow do something different, as if we hadn't done what we did. When God sees what we will do, he sees our behavior as it is. Your question implies that we have the option of doing something other than what we already did. But we don't. It's like the idea that you can't unsay what you've said. If you call someone stupid, or fat, or ugly, thereby hurting their feelings, you can apologize, but you can't unsay what you said. You said it, and it is a done deal. Human actions in the time-space continuum are like that. When you do something, you have done it. That's it. It's a done deal. It can't happen differently—not because God has seen it, but because what he saw is what you did. You didn't do something else; you did what you did."

Nodding, Susan said, "Okay. I think I see what you're saying. This turned out to be a lot more complicated than I thought it was going to be."

"Life is like that sometimes."

"Is there anything else you can think of that I need to know about all of this?"

"Yes. One other thing: understanding human free will impacts how we pray."

That appeared to surprise her.

"How?"

"Have you ever prayed a prayer that involved you asking God to make someone stop doing a hurtful thing?"

"Yeah. Last year I was dating a guy that drank too much. When he did, he'd get mean. At the time, I thought I loved him. And when he wasn't drinking, he was a wonderful guy. But alcohol in his system changed him. It was like Dr. Jekyll and Mr. Hyde. So I prayed for him, asking God to make him stop drinking."

"Given our discussion this morning, do you see a problem with that?"

She thought for a moment and nodded. "Since Dave has free will, God can't make him do anything. I was asking God to do something that he couldn't do."

"Yeah, you were. Lots of people ask God to do things he can't do. And then, when he doesn't do what they asked, they get angry with him. Or at least they get confused, and wonder why he didn't do anything."

"Kind of puts God in a tough spot, doesn't it?"

"It does," I said.

Susan drained her coffee cup and said, "You know, I didn't really know what to expect when I agree to come here and talk with you. But this has been both interesting and helpful. Thank you."

"My pleasure. Come again, and we'll talk some more."

Chapter 4
Mike and the Identity of Jesus

"Are you Dr. Baker?" he asked. He was a big guy. Six-five, maybe. Two-forty. All muscle. Looked to be in his early twenties. He had a cup of coffee in his hand.

"I am," I said.

He extended his hand. "I'm Mike Garvey. Conner said you'd be here and that you could help me."

"I'll give it my best shot. Sit down."

"Thanks. Conner was going to come with me, but he got an emergency call from a client and had to go get someone's computer system back online."

"I understand."

"He said you used to be a professor."

"That's right."

"And that you also used to be a missionary and before that a minister."

"Guilty on all counts."

"He said you'd be able to answer my question."

"Maybe," I said. "Depends on the question. Before we get started, though, I need to refill my coffee and get a scone. I'm hungry today. You want a scone to go with you coffee?"

"I don't know. Never had a scone."

"They're pretty good. A cross between a biscuit and a donut."

"I like biscuits and donuts," Mike said. "So, sure. Thanks."

When I returned to the table with the scones and fresh coffee, Mike said, "I hope you don't mind me coming here like this."

"Not at all. I do this sort of thing all the time. It's one of the reasons I come here every day. Try your scone."

Mike took a bite and nodded. "Good," he said around the scone in his mouth.

I took a bite of mine, had a sip of coffee, and said, "Okay, so how can I help you?"

"I wasn't raised with any kind of religion," he said. "My parents weren't anti-religion or anything, they just weren't interested. I go to school down in Austin. Got a football scholarship. I met a girl there. She's a Christian. Very committed. Got me interested in it. I've been going to church with her, and I like it. I've learned some good stuff. But I took a class in comparative religions. Mostly I took it just because it fit into my schedule. But I thought I'd learn some stuff that I could talk to Karen about. That's my girlfriend. But it didn't work out like that. The professor was very anti-Christian. He seemed okay with all the other religions we talked about, but he really didn't like Christianity. And he seemed to have a real problem with

Jesus, especially the part about Jesus being God incarnate. He raised some questions about Jesus' identity that I couldn't answer. Said Jesus was just a Jewish guy from a poor family who was trying to make a name for himself. Said he was smart enough to fool his followers into thinking he was the Messiah. So they told a bunch of stories about him that weren't true but that people believed anyway. And so a myth about him developed, and people believed it."

"And you want to know if that's true," I said.

"Yes. I mean, I believe in Jesus. Or at least I want to. But this guy said some stuff that I can't answer, so I'm really confused."

"Have you talked with Karen about your concerns?"

"No. She'd be upset. And I don't know if she'd understand or not."

"Okay," I said. "I understand what you're struggling with. Let's see if we can't help you out with this."

We paused to eat some more of our scones and drink some coffee. Then I said, "Okay, the first thing you have to do is decide whether or not you believe the Bible is a divinely inspired book—God's communication to human beings."

"I guess so. Yeah."

"You don't sound like you're sure."

"Well, I don't know. I mean how do you ever know for sure?"

"There are two different bases for certainty: empirical evidence, and rationalistic evidence. Empirical evidence is evidence you experience with your physical senses: you see something, hear something, smell something, taste something, or touch or feel something. And because of

57

having experienced it with your senses, you have certain knowledge regarding that thing. I'm sitting on this chair. Therefore, I know it will support my weight because I'm sitting on it, and it is, in fact, supporting my weight. I have empirical knowledge of the fact that the chair will support my weight."

"Okay, sure."

"But certainty can also be arrived at rationally."

"I'm not sure I know what that means."

"It means you don't have to have physical sensory experience to be sure of something."

"How you gonna be sure of it?"

"Fair question. What is a brother?"

"A brother?"

"Yes. Technically. What is the definition of the word brother?"

He got out his phone and looked it up. I smiled. I guess he figured I wanted an exact definition.

"A male sibling," Mike said.

"Correct. So if I say, *all brothers are male*, how would you know that that is true?"

He looked at me for a long moment. Finally, he said, "You mean without having to go around and check each one to see if he is a male?"

"Yes."

"Well, I guess you'd know because a brother is a male sibling. If someone is a brother, he is a male."

"Exactly. So all brothers are male. You know that because you know what a brother is. You don't need empirical evidence. You have rational evidence—the concept and meaning of the word brother. Works the same

58

way with *all sisters are female*. Or *there are no married bachelors*."

"So you're saying that for some things, you don't need actual physical evidence to know something, to be certain. You can just think about it and figure it out and be certain."

"Yes."

"And you're suggesting that I can do that with Jesus' identity?"

"Yes."

"Okay, I'm willing to give it a try, but I have no idea how."

"Okay, so we begin with the Bible itself. It claims to be inspired by God. In other words, God was guiding the human authors in communicating his message to human beings."

"Okay. But how do you know it really is God's message?"

"Exactly. How do you know? There is no physical evidence that proves it, so we approach the question rationally."

Mike nodded.

"Is there anything you can think of in the Bible that would demonstrate that it is not merely the work of the human authors?"

"I don't know."

"What about fulfilled prophecy?"

"I guess. Maybe."

"There are about 2500 prophecies in the Bible. Many of them are very specific about things God will do. Lots of them, well over 100, are about Jesus. Some of them were given hundreds of years before he was born and are very specific about different features of his life. They include things he could not have manipulated. How do you account for that if the authors are just some Jewish guys making stuff up?"

"I don't know."

"You can't. The only way to account for fulfilled prophecy in the Bible is that the authors were being guided by God in what they wrote. There's no other way they could have known things that were hundreds of years in the future."

"Okay. I see that."

"So when the Bible says Jesus is God incarnate, if you believe the Bible is a divinely inspired book, you accept that as true."

"So, because the Bible says so, you believe it?"

"Partly, yes."

"Partly," Mike said. "What's the other part?"

I paused for some more of my scone and a sip of coffee. So did Mike.

"The other part to help you make up your mind about who Jesus was is the content and impact of his teaching. One of the things the people of Jesus' day noticed about his teaching was that it was not like the teaching of the rabbis. Jesus spoke with a certainty and authority the rabbis did not have. His focus was different. His way of teaching was different. The content of his teaching was different. When people encountered Jesus, their consensus was, *He's different*. People came by the thousands to hear Jesus because he taught them things no one else was teaching."

"Like what?" Mike asked.

"Jesus taught people practical things that helped them live better lives, that helped them interact with other people more effectively. For instance, he taught people to treat other people the way they wanted to be treated. *Do unto others as you would have them do unto you.* It's a simple formula. But think how much better the world would be if everyone followed that simple rule: *treat other people the way you want them to treat you.*"

"Okay, so Jesus was a really good teacher who taught really important stuff. But that doesn't mean he is God incarnate."

"No, it doesn't. But it suggests that there was something special about him."

"Maybe. There's gotta be more than that though, right?"

"There is," I said. "The miracles Jesus performed provide evidence of his identity."

"Miracles," Mike said.

"The miracles Jesus did are pretty good evidence."

"He healed a lot of people," Mike said. "Did some amazing things. Does that make him God?"

"He healed the sick. He gave sight to the blind, hearing to the deaf. Healed crippled people so they could walk. Drove demons from people. On more than one occasion raised the dead. He calmed a storm at sea, walked on water, turned water to wine, fed thousands of people with only a loaf of bread and a few fish. He performed more miracles of different kinds than anyone else in history."

"But how can we be sure he really did those things?" Mike asked.

"Because people who saw what he did told us about them."

"Can we trust their account of what happened?"

"That question goes back to what you believe about the Bible in general. Did the biblical authors lie about what they saw? Were they intending to deceive or mislead people? Or were they just so dumb that they misinterpreted what they saw. The blind man who became able to see wasn't really blind. The deaf man wasn't really deaf. The dead girl, the dead boy, and the dead man weren't really dead."

Mike was thinking about it.

"Either Jesus' followers saw what they saw, or they were confused, or they lied. Or, they were telling the truth, and Jesus did amazing things: including walking on water and raising the dead. And if you'll notice, the people today who claim to be working miracles—none of them are walking on water, turning water to wine, giving sight to the blind, or raising the dead. The kind of miracles Jesus did are not being done by people today."

"That's true," Mike said.

"And then, of course, there is the resurrection of Jesus."

"Okay," Mike said. "I've heard a couple of sermons about that. Why is Jesus' resurrection so special? I mean he wasn't the first person to be resurrected. I mean he brought people back to life, right?"

"He did," I said. "Jesus' resurrection is different because he was resurrected directly by God and ascended back to heaven forty days later. The other people who were resurrected lived to die again. But Jesus rose from the grave never to die again. His resurrection was a victory over death."

"But how do we know that he really was resurrected?"

"Lots of people were eyewitnesses to the event."

"And their testimony is trustworthy?"

"Well, they were Jesus' followers. They knew him well. One of the women saw him in the garden where the tomb was. All of his apostles saw him on multiple occasions, interacted with him, and ate with him. Then a group of over five hundred of his followers saw him. That's a lot of eyewitnesses."

"Yeah, but how do we know they actually saw what they think they saw? Or that they didn't make it up?"

"You mean lie."

"You have to admit that it is at least a possibility."

"Sure. And it is also possible that Tinker Bell could fly in here and sprinkle us with pixie dust so we could all fly off with her to Never-Never Land where we would never have to grow up."

I couldn't tell if what I'd said confused or offended Mike, so I said, "Look, given what the apostles did over the rest of their lives, what they taught, what they sacrificed, what they accomplished, how they died, what others had to say about them, the idea that they lied about Jesus' resurrection is as remote as what I just said about Tinker Bell. Jesus had at least one hundred and twenty followers in Jerusalem after his death and resurrection. Hard to get that many people to participate in a lie. They had all, no doubt, gone to see the empty tomb. Jesus had spoken about his death and resurrection. He prophesied it. And the prophets of old, hundreds of years earlier, had prophesied his death. It was all part of God's plan for how he was going to save humanity from the consequences of their sins. God himself would become a human being and offer himself as a sacrifice for sin, so human sin could be forgiven. God loved his human children enough to die for them so they wouldn't have to bear the punishment for their sins. That's what Jesus' death and resurrection was all about. If God can create the universe, is it too much to imagine that he could become a human being, sacrifice himself, and raise himself from the dead?"

"Wait a minute. A few minutes ago you said that God raised Jesus from the dead. Now you're saying that God became a human being, died, and raised himself from the dead."

"Yes."

"Well, which is it? It can't be both."

"Sure it can. It depends on how you are looking at it. Most people tend to think of Jesus as a separate person from God. But if Jesus is God incarnate, then Jesus is God. God is Jesus. So, while you can say that God raised Jesus from the dead, since Jesus is God in human form, God raised himself from the dead."

"It gets kind of confusing," Mike said.

"Perhaps. But like I said, if God can create the universe, is it so hard to believe that he could become a human being and offer himself as a sacrifice of atonement?"

I waited for Mike to answer.

"No, I guess not," he said after a moment.

"Mike, what it boils down to is that either you believe in God as creator and savior, or you don't. All of it makes sense, and there's plenty of evidence to support the story. There will always be people who deny and ridicule it. But the evidence is clear. You have the eyewitness account of over five hundred people who saw Jesus alive after his death. Jesus rose from the grave. And he did it so you and I could be forgiven and enjoy a relationship with him."

Mike was nodding. "Yeah. He did. I know he did. That professor just kind of screwed me up. Asked some questions that I couldn't answer. But you answered them. Thanks, Dr. Baker."

"Glad I could help."

"If I have more questions, can I come talk to you again?"

"Absolutely. With or without Conner."

Chapter 5
Jim And Why Jesus Had To Die

"The whole thing's a bloody mess," Jim said. "The Old Testament, the New Testament. Blood everywhere. Why did there have to be so much death and blood for God to save humanity?"

"Jim's a little upset," Conner said to me.

"I see that," I said.

"You'll have to forgive him. He thinks God could have come up with a way to save people without so much death and blood being part of the plan."

"I understand," I said to Conner. Then, to Jim I said, "You can take comfort in the fact that lots of people, including plenty of biblical scholars, have wondered the same thing."

"So, what's the answer?" Jim said. "Why does the whole thing have to involve so much death and blood?"

"There are, I think, two reasons. The first reason is to illustrate how horrible and ugly sin is—so horrible and so ugly that it required blood and death to resolve the problem.

People tend to want to minimize sin. '*So, I did ... (whatever, fill in the blank) It's not that big a deal. Plenty of other people have done the same thing.*' So, the first reason is to show that sin is a big deal. The second reason is because when God began trying to help his people understand how the problem of sin was ultimately going to be resolved, the beliefs and practices of religion throughout the known world at that time involved a lot of blood and death."

"I'm not sure I understand either of those two things," Jim said.

"Don't feel bad. You're not alone."

Conner said, "I get the feeling this is not going to be a short conversation. I'll go get us some coffee."

While Conner was gone, Jim said, "I'm sorry if I sounded angry."

"Don't worry about it. You sounded like someone who was really frustrated about something that was important to him. Nothing wrong with that."

"I need to make sense of this," he said. "It seems to me that Christianity is either the best thing to ever come along, or it is one giant fraud. To me, the message of love, and mercy, and forgiveness, and hope, and relationship with God is great. And I want all of that. But it seems like it's all predicated on blood and death and ugliness. I just don't understand why God couldn't have found another way to accomplish his purpose than to become a human being and suffer and die."

Conner returned with coffee. He had also bought scones, which was nice because I hadn't had one yet, and I was hungry. We took a moment to sample the coffee and scones. Good. Then I said, "What you're asking is a valid question. I hope I can give you an explanation that will satisfy you."

Jim nodded as he chewed a bite of his scone.

"I think the best place to begin is with the idea that God was trying to communicate some important and challenging ideas to ancient people whose assumptions about spiritual things often got in the way of their understanding what the truth really was. In other words, they had all kinds of goofy beliefs that God needed to work around if he was going to help them understand the truth."

"Like what?" Jim asked.

"Well, for one, pretty much all ancient people had a negative view of the gods or God. They feared them. To be in the presence of a god meant you were going to die. The gods were always angry, just a heartbeat away from bringing destruction on everyone. Sacrifices were believed to appease the wrath of the gods. Offering a sacrifice of something very valuable was a way to get on the good side of whichever god you worshiped. The sacrifice of an animal was thought to be a great sacrifice that would cause the god to bless you. So, long before the one true God began trying to help the Hebrews understand what they needed to know, the Hebrews believed basically what most other cultural groups believed—that they had to offer sacrifices to gain God's favor."

"And that wasn't correct?" Jim asked.

"No, it wasn't. God has always been favorably disposed toward his human children. He loves us. Unconditionally. We don't have to earn his love by offering sacrifices."

"So why did he set up a system of sacrifices?"

"He needed the people to understand how horrible sin is and what it takes to get rid of it—blood, death. And since people at that time thought in terms of animal sacrifice, he used a practice that already existed, that they already understood. He added new meaning to it, but he used a practice that was already part of the cultures of the ancient world."

"So he didn't invent it."

"No, he didn't."

"But why did he use a system like that? Why not come up with something different? Something less bloody?"

"I suspect that you are missing some important information. Are you aware that after an animal was slaughtered and offered as a sacrifice, that only the blood and in some cases the entrails were actually offered as the sacrifice? The meat of the animal was eaten."

"I didn't know that."

"In ancient Israel, aside from one very special kind of sacrifice where the entire animal was offered, only the blood and entrails were offered, and the meat was eaten. Half of it was eaten by the family who offered the sacrifice, and half of it was donated to the temple for the priest to eat. So the millions of animals that were sacrificed over the centuries would have been slaughtered anyway to provide meat for the family."

"So they weren't just killing them to offer to God."

"Well, they were, but the meat was eaten."

"I guess that makes a difference."

"God used an existing practice to teach the people an important spiritual truth."

"How terrible sin is."

"Yes. And what it takes to get rid of sin."

"Death," Jim said.

"Yes."

"But why?" Jim asked. "I mean, God is God. Couldn't he have just forgiven them and been done with it?"

"No."

"No? Why not? God can do whatever he wants."

"No, he can't," I said.

That idea backed Jim up a bit.

"What do you mean he can't do whatever he wants?"

"For God to be God," I said, "he has to be perfect in every way. His actions and behaviors must be consistent with his nature."

"Okay."

"Dealing with human sin is not only a matter of love, but also a matter of justice."

"Justice," Jim said.

"Yes. Laws had been violated. Rules had been broken. If God simply overlooked those violations, he would not be acting in a just manner. For God to be perfect in justice, a penalty had to be paid. Someone had to be punished. But God did not want to punish all of his human children. He loved them and wanted to forgive them. But his divine nature—perfection in every way in all things—would not allow him to simply ignore the fact that laws had been broken. Justice is as important as love. Before he could forgive individuals for their transgressions, someone had to be punished in order to satisfy the demands of justice."

"I never thought of justice as being that important," Jim said.

"It is. So, God's plan, a plan that satisfied the demands of justice and of love, involved God becoming a human being in the person of Jesus, and sacrificing himself. Although he had not sinned and did not deserve to be punished, he took the punishment that we deserved upon himself, being punished in our place, so he could then forgive us for the evil things we had done. Jesus' death on the cross was the perfect combination of justice and love. It satisfied the demands of justice and of love."

"Okay," Jim said, "I think I see what you're saying, but I'm a little confused about some of the language you're using."

"Which part?"

"This thing about God in the person of Jesus. Some of what you are saying sounds like you are saying God and Jesus are the same person. And that it was God who died on the cross."

"It was."

"How can God die?"

"In the incarnation, when God became a human being in the person of Jesus, he did not become less God; his divine nature was not minimized in any way. He was still one hundred percent God. What happened was he acquired a new, additional nature, so that in addition to being one hundred percent God, he was also one hundred percent human. He became a God-person, a two hundred percent being: fully God, and fully human. This human-God was known as Jesus. It was this human part of God that died on the cross."

"So the human part of God died, but the divine part didn't."

71

"Correct."

"I don't understand that."

"Yeah, I know," I said. "The nature of God can be confusing."

"Yeah, well, it's frustrating. Why can't God explain himself any better than that?"

"Because it would be like explaining quantum physics to a two year old."

Jim frowned, and said, "Meaning the concept of God is beyond us?"

"Way beyond us."

"So, how are we supposed to believe in something we can't understand?"

"That's a good question. And it's why God uses so many different metaphors to describe himself and our relationship with him."

"You mean like father, and shepherd, and king, and all that."

"Yes."

Jim took a moment to drink some of his coffee and organize his thoughts. "Okay," he said. "Let me see if I've got this straight. God became a human being and let people kill him so he could forgive them for their sins, one of which was killing him."

"Basically, yes. If the people would turn from their sinful ways and accept Jesus as their savior, he would forgive them."

"Don't take this the wrong way," Jim said, "but is there something in the Bible that explains all this?"

"Sure. You got a Bible app on your phone?"

"Yeah."

"Look up Romans 3:21-26. Read it out loud."

Jim found the text and began: *"But now a righteousness from God, apart from the law, has been made known, to which the Law and the Prophets testify. This righteousness from God comes through faith in Jesus Christ to all who believe. There is no difference, for all have sinned and fall short of the glory of God, and are justified freely by his grace through the redemption that came by Jesus Christ. God presented him as a sacrifice of atonement, through faith in his blood. He did this to demonstrate his justice, because in his forbearance he had left the sins committed beforehand unpunished—he did it to demonstrate his justice at the present time, so as to be just and the one who justifies those who have faith in Jesus."*

"Good," I said. "In verse 25, in the phrase *sacrifice of atonement*, the word *atonement* is from a Greek word that means *propitiation*. It is the idea that the sacrifice God offered took away God's anger at sin. It placated him. But the crucial idea in the text is that since Jesus was God incarnate, God offered himself as a sacrifice to himself. And by sacrificing himself in the person of Jesus, he placated himself. He did for us what we could not do for ourselves."

"But the way it is worded," Jim said, "makes it sound like God and Jesus are two separate people, or beings or whatever."

"It does. The language is a continuation of the father-son metaphor that God used to help the people understand a reality that otherwise would have been beyond them."

"That's a lot to process," Jim said.

"It is. But I have confidence you can do it."

"Maybe. But I'm not sure I see the connection between Jesus' death and all the lambs and goats and other animals killed in the Old Testament. I understand what you said about the meat of the animal being eaten and all, but if God was going to become human and offer himself as a sacrifice, why have all those animal sacrifices?"

"Everything done under the old, Mosaic covenant, the Old Testament Law, was designed to serve as a foreshadowing of what would happen in the establishing of the New Covenant."

"Foreshadowing."

"Yes. A symbolic event or ritual that happens before the actual event. You see, the symbolic representation that occurs before the actual event points forward in time to the actual event. It uses something the people understand, in this case sacrificing an animal as an offering for one's sin, to symbolically represent the actual event, in this case, the sacrifice of Jesus and the forgiveness they enjoy because of it."

"So, you're saying that if God had simply said that one day he would become a human and offer himself in sacrifice for sin, the people would not have understood."

"Yes."

"Why not? It seems straightforward enough."

"Because in ancient times people had so many mistaken ideas about God and his relationship with humans that there was no way they could make sense out of the idea of the incarnation and a divinely offered sacrifice of atonement."

Jim was frowning as he sipped his coffee, still struggling with the idea.

"An important part of all of it," I said, "was the idea of the substitutionary nature of the sacrifice."

"Substitutionary," Jim repeated.

"Sure. Think about it. The lamb or goat had not sinned. Why did it have to die?"

"That's what I've been asking."

"The person offering the animal had sinned and deserved to be punished. The punishment for sin is death. If everyone had gotten what he or she deserved, everyone would have been killed. But God didn't want all his human children to be killed. So he allowed an animal to be substituted, to take the place of the guilty person. The blood, the life, of the animal was substituted for that of the guilty person."

"So then why not just continue on with that system?"

"Because the blood of the animal could not really atone for human sin. Human sin required human blood, a human life, for the demands of justice to be satisfied."

"So, that's why God became a human and offered himself—human blood, a human life offered for human sin."

"Exactly."

Jim took a deep breath and leaned back in his chair. He sipped his coffee, nodded, and said, "Yeah, I get it now. I see what you're saying."

I took the last swig of my coffee and said, "It's complicated, but it is understandable."

"Thank you, Dr. Baker. This helps a lot."

Conner was smiling. "It was an excellent explanation," he said. "Helped me out, too. I hadn't heard that part about pro ... Propit ... What'd you call it?"

"Propitiation."

"Yeah. Propitiation. I like that. I'm gonna do some additional research on that."

Jim stood and shook my hand. "Thanks again, Doc. I appreciate it."

"My pleasure."

Chapter 6
Shannon and the Origin of Evil

"Dr. Baker," Conner said, "this is my friend Shannon. She's also one of my clients."

I stood and shook her hand.

"Conner takes care of my internet stuff," Shannon said. "And one day while he was in my office, we got to talking about evil."

"And she had some questions that I couldn't answer," Conner said. "But I told her that I had a friend who could."

"I'll do my best," I said. "What questions do you have about evil?"

"Where it came from," she said. "The only answer I can come up with is that God created it. But that doesn't feel right. Conner said you could explain it."

"Let's jump into it," I said, "And see what happens. Any place in particular you'd like to begin?"

"Not really," Shannon said. "I just want to know if God created evil, and if not, where did it come from?"

"You want the long answer or the short answer?"

"Short."

"No, God didn't create evil. Evil, as a concept, has always existed."

The blank look on her face was not promising. I waited. Conner waited. Finally, Shannon said, "I guess I'm gong to need the long answer."

I smiled. "Complete explanations are usually more helpful," I said. I sipped some of my coffee. "Okay, what are your assumptions about God and creation?"

"My assumptions," she said, sounding uncertain. "Well, I guess if you mean what I think about the question, I assume that since God created everything, he must have created evil, because evil is part of everything. But if he did, doesn't that make him responsible for all the evil in the world? It seems like it would, but that doesn't seem right. I mean, it doesn't make any sense. So, where did evil come from? Did Satan create it? Satan is evil, so maybe he created evil. But then, wouldn't that make Satan sort of equal with God? I don't know. It's all very confusing."

"It's confusing for a lot of people," I said. "Let's see if we can't make it a little less confusing."

"Okay."

"What is evil?"

"What is evil? I don't know. People doing bad things I guess."

"People do lots of things. Are all of them evil?"

"No, of course not."

"So only some of the things people do are evil."

"Yes."

"Which ones?"

"You mean which things are evil?"

"Yes."

"I don't know. The things that hurt people, I suppose."

"Does that mean that you are not sure which things are evil or why we consider them evil?"

Frowning, Shannon said, "I didn't realize I was going to have to answer this many questions."

"Okay, maybe walking you through the whole thing is not a good idea. So, let's approach it more straightforwardly—though there will still be some questions. Is there a difference between the actions we define as evil and the concept of evil?"

Apparently, Shannon wasn't used to this sort of thinking. After a moment, she said, "I'm not sure."

"Actions are things we do. They are concrete. Concepts are abstract ideas. What do you do with concepts or ideas?"

"Think about them?" she said uncertainly.

"Exactly. Now, what is the relationship between an action and what you think about that action?"

"Well, one is what you did or do, and the other is what you think about it."

"Meaning, in the context of this discussion, why you define it as either good or evil?"

"Yes."

"So, are the doing and the thinking two completely separate things?"

"Seems like it," Shannon said.

"Seems like it?"

"Okay, yes," she said. "They're different things. How you think about a thing and doing that thing, are two different things."

"Yes, they are. Now, when you are brushing your teeth in the morning, and you spit in the sink, is that a bad thing? Is it evil?"

"No."

"What about walking up to someone and spitting on them? Would that be evil?"

"Yes."

"Why?"

"Because it's an ugly thing to do. It's disrespectful. It's disgusting."

"Why is it not ugly and disgusting when you spit your toothpaste into the sink, but it is ugly and disgusting when you spit on a person?"

She sipped her coffee and thought for a moment. "Because of what it means when you spit on a person."

"Yes. Because we assign meanings to behaviors. Smiling at someone is a good thing, spitting on them is a bad thing. But whether a given action is considered good or bad is related to the meaning we attach to it."

"Okay, I see that."

"Is giving someone a thumbs up a good thing?"

"Sure."

"How about giving them the finger?"

"That's not a good thing."

"Why not? What's the difference between the two actions?"

"Because one means something good and the other one doesn't."

"Yes. Actions or behaviors are concrete things to which we assign meanings. The meanings are …?"

"Umm."

"What would you identify them as?"

After a few seconds, Shannon said, "Ideas."

"Yes. They are abstract ideas or concepts regarding the nature of actual things that happen."

"Okay, I get that," Shannon said, "but I'm not seeing what it has to do with where evil came from."

"The point is that evil is a reality that exists at two levels: the concrete level—things we do, and the abstract or conceptual level—how we think about or categorize those things. There is actual evil that hurts people, and there is conceptual evil that is an idea that exists in relation to it's opposite, that is in relation to good. Evil and good. At the conceptual level, they are how we categorize behaviors."

"Okay," Shannon said.

"Which one came first," I asked, "actual evil or conceptual evil?"

"I have no idea."

"Okay, if we think in terms of God and creation, when could actual evil have begun?"

She thought about it. "When there were people around to do bad things."

"What about before people were created?"

"Are you saying people created evil?"

"No. Not at all. And you have to resist the temptation to jump ahead. The question is, what was the reality related to evil before beings existed to do evil?"

"I don't know."

"What kind of a being is God?"

"What *kind* of a being is God?"

"Yes."

"I don't know."

I was going too deep, too fast. "Okay," I said, "since we haven't had that discussion, that's probably an unfair question. In the stuff I've written about God, I describe him as the eternally existing rational mind."

"Okay," she said. "I've never heard God explained like that before, but I get what you are saying. He's always existed, and he's rational.

"Yes. And if that's the case, we can define God as a *thinking being*. Whatever else he is, fundamentally he is a thinking being. And as such, he thinks. Minds think. And rational minds think abstract thoughts. Would you agree?"

"I guess. Sure."

"Before God created people who could do evil, could God have thought about good and evil?"

"Seems like he would have been able to."

"Of course, he could. The eternally existing rational mind could think about anything it wanted to think about, including the ideas of good and evil. So, at a conceptual level, evil existed in contrast to good for as long as the eternally existing mind existed to think about it."

"So you're saying that if God always existed, then the ideas or concepts he thought about also always existed."

"Yes."

"So evil, as a concept, always existed."

"Yes."

"Couldn't you just have said that?"

I laughed. "I suppose I could have. But I thought it was important to help you think about the answer instead of just giving you the answer."

"Like my mom telling me to look up how a word was spelled instead of telling me how to spell it."

I smiled and sipped my coffee.

"Okay," Shannon said. "I get it. Someday when I have kids and they ask me how to spell a word, I'll probably tell them to go look it up."

I nodded and drank some more coffee.

"But what I'm not sure I get is how evil as a concept that God thought about is related to actual evil that people do."

"Good question," I said. "Abstract evil vs. actual evil. Are they the same or different?"

"Seems to me they're different. One is real, the other isn't."

"Like a photograph of a person isn't the person?"

"Yes," she said. "Exactly."

"Granted. A photograph of a person isn't the person. But when you are dealing with concepts and actions related to those concepts, is it the case that they are completely different?"

"I don't know."

"If we say helping the needy is good, and then you help the needy, have you done a good thing?"

"Yes."

"So, what's the connection between the way we define or understand a thing and the thing itself? Is there a connection?"

"Well, sure. There would be a connection."

"But they are still not the same thing," I said. "So, for instance, you could ask yourself what kind of an act would it be to teach someone who couldn't read to read. And you might think that it would be a good thing. So you categorize teaching an illiterate person how to read as a good thing. But categorizing it as a good thing and actually teaching someone how to read are two different things."

"Yes."

"And so," I said, "it would work the other way around as well. You could decide that spitting in someone's face is a bad thing, but categorizing it as such is not the same as doing it."

"Right."

"Okay, then, so God, as the eternally existing rational mind, contemplated good and evil as concepts, and perhaps even thought of specific examples of how the concepts might be acted out in a physical context, he was not actually doing good or evil. He was contemplating the ideas of good and evil."

"Okay."

"So good and evil existed conceptually."

"I guess."

"So then God," I said, "creates humans, and in time, humans do things that are good and that are evil. Because God created humans who did evil, did God create evil?"

Shannon sipped her coffee as she considered my question. "If evil," she said, "already existed at the conceptual level, and had always existed at that level, then no, God did not create evil when he created humans. But if actual evil hadn't been done, then ..."

I completed her thought for her. "Then weren't humans responsible for making conceptual evil an actual thing in the physical world?"

"Yeah," she said. "I probably wouldn't have said it just like that, but yeah, that's what I was trying to say."

"And it's a good question. The answer, I think, is because humans did actual evil things doesn't mean they created evil. It simply means that they did things that were defined as evil."

"So because conceptual evil always existed, actual evil did too, even though it hadn't been done yet?"

"Yes."

"Hmm," she said. "That's an interesting idea. But it makes me wonder about something else."

"What?" I asked.

"Why did God create people who would do evil?"

"Good question."

"Do you have an answer?" she said.

"I think I do."

Conner smiled. "He's got an answer for everything," he said.

"No, I don't," I said. "There's lots of stuff for which I have no explanation. It's just that I've spent a lot of time thinking about these sorts of questions."

"Okay," Shannon said. "So what's the answer?"

"God created people who were capable of doing evil because he wanted other beings around who were the same kind of thinking beings he was, so he and they could enjoy a mutually satisfying relationship."

"What?"

"Are you a dog person?"

85

"Yeah, I love dogs."

"Me, too. I've got a Rottweiler named Worf. Amazing dog. I love him. But I can't have the same kind of a relationship with him as I can have with another human being. Why not?"

"Because Worf is a dog, and as amazing as dogs are, they are not capable of the kind of relationship humans are capable of."

"Exactly. An intimate relationship—and when I say intimate I'm not talking about sexual intimacy, but intimacy in general. Closeness. Sharing. That sort of thing—an intimate relationship requires a level of sameness. Beings that are of the same sort can enjoy a relationship that beings and creatures—different species—cannot enjoy."

"Sure. I get that."

"So, God created humans in his image, that is, created them as the same kind of a being he is so he and they could enjoy a mutually satisfying relationship."

"So humans are the same kind of beings God is?"

"Fundamentally, yes."

"So humans are like little gods?"

"I wouldn't say that, exactly. What I mean is that God is fundamentally a rational mind, a thinking kind of a being. So are we. We are embodied; he is not. He has always existed, but we began to exist only a short time ago. Because he has always existed, he knows things we do not, and he is very powerful. We are not very powerful because we are only baby minds. But fundamentally, we are the same kinds of beings—thinking beings. Just like a human baby is fundamentally the same kind of a being its parents are, even though it is not capable of thinking much of anything while it is still an infant, it is still a thinking being."

"So, we're like baby gods?"

"Well, I try to avoid identifying humans as gods. But I'm comfortable saying that we are baby minds. God is the eternally existing rational mind, while we are baby minds."

"I see," she said. "But what has that got to do with humans being capable of doing evil?"

"Since humans are created in God's image, we are rational beings like he is. Part of being rational is being self-aware, very highly aware. We are so highly aware that we are aware that we are aware. And because we are, we are aware that alternatives exist and that we can choose one alternative over another. Because we are self-aware, we are also self-determined. We are aware of alternatives, and we choose one alternative over another. Self-awareness and self-determination are the results of being rational."

"And because humans are self-determined," Shannon said, "they can choose to do either good or evil."

"Yes."

She thought about that for a moment. "But couldn't God keep people from deciding to do evil?"

"Can God make a round square?"

"A round square?"

"Yeah. Can God make a round square? Or a square circle?"

"Well, no."

"That's right. And neither can he make a rational being that is self-determined who is not free to choose good or evil."

"So God has to allow people to do as they please, even if pain and suffering are the result?"

"Yes."

"That's got to be frustrating for God."

"I'm sure it is."

"So, God did not create evil, It always existed as a concept. When humans, who are self-determined, chose to do evil, conceptual evil became actual evil. And since God made people as self-determined beings, he must allow them to choose freely between good and evil."

"Sounds like you've got a handle on it."

Shannon drained the last of her coffee from her cup and said, "This has been so much more than I expected it would be. Thank you."

"Glad you found it helpful."

Chapter 7
Diane and the Need for Organized Religion

"No," Diane said. "It's not that I have anything against the church *per se*. I don't think the church is bad or anything like that. It's just that it seems unnecessary to me. The times I've gone, it didn't seem to be relevant to me. It didn't have anything to offer."

"I see," I said. "And what are you thinking I can do for you?"

"Actually," she said, "it's what Conner thinks you can do for me. He believes you can help me see that organized religion is, in his words, both necessary and meaningful."

I looked at Conner. "So you make the claim, and I have to support it."

He smiled. "You can do it better than I can."

"I see," I said. "Okay, Diane, is there a specific question you want to start with?"

"Not really. I've told you what I think. So as I see it, it's your turn to convince me otherwise."

I liked her. She was one of those petite cuties whose personality was bigger than she was.

"Okay," I said, "then let's start with what the church is."

She nodded, looking open and interested, and took a sip of her coffee.

"The English word church," I said, "comes from a Greek word that means assembly. The idea is that Christians assemble together to worship God. But when you look closely at the concept of the church in the New Testament you see that it includes the idea of a community of believers who love each other and interact like a family. The church is the family of God. God is the father; Christians are his children, brothers and sisters who care about and help each other. The weekly assembly, the church service, is like a weekly father's day gathering where God's children come together to honor and worship him."

"Every week?"

"Every week. But there's more going on," I said, "than simply worshiping God. Another reason believers come together is to remember Jesus' death and resurrection, to focus on what he did for us, and to thank him. We do that during the Lord's Supper, or Communion, part of the assembly."

"And those things can't be done by an individual wherever he or she is?"

"Some people like to think so, but a healthy relationship requires togetherness, interaction, and not just with God, but with other Christians. And living the Christian life successfully is not an easy thing to do. One of the purposes of the weekly gathering is for individual believers to find the support and encouragement they need to face the challenges of faithful Christian living."

"I've been to lots of church services," Diane said. "Didn't find them all that helpful."

"Then I would suggest that one of two things is wrong: either you've been attending churches where something is amiss in that church, or your attitude and expectations need adjusting."

"So it's my fault?"

"Might be. I don't know. Over the years, I've found that if someone goes to church with the idea of *getting something out of it*, they are usually disappointed."

"Why else would someone go? You said one of the purposes was to get support and encouragement."

"Yes. But what you get, what you walk away with, depends a great deal on what you bring to the experience."

"What am I supposed to bring?"

"A grateful heart of adoration."

"What? I … what does that mean? I don't understand."

"When you come to God through faith in Jesus, acknowledging your sinfulness, and asking for forgiveness, he accepts you and forgives you, making it possible for you to enjoy a relationship with him. If you understand what your condition was before that—separated from God and hopelessly lost—you have a deep appreciation for what he did for you. You love him. You want to develop a deeper intimacy with him. And when you worship in an assembly of people who love him and enjoy their relationship with him, there's a benefit to be enjoyed. If you simply go to church because you are supposed to, or if you go looking for some magical feeling of mystical delight, you will be disappointed. If you go to honor and adore your savior, you will find a sense of joy in knowing you are part of a community of saved people who look forward to eternity in a wonderful relationship with God. And in that you find the courage to face the challenges of life because you know God is there to help you."

"And you don't think I can do or get any of that on my own."

I smiled and sipped my coffee. "Humans are relational beings," I said. "When you see someone living all by themselves with no contact with other people, you know that something has gone terribly wrong for them. Humans need relationships with other people. We seek out people to be with, to live life with. We need someone to love and to love us. It's part of our human nature, part of who we are. Understanding that basic human need, God established the church to provide relationships, to provide a community of people who share a common faith, common values, common goals, who have the same weaknesses with which they need help, the same problems for which they need solutions, the same needs to be satisfied. To be a dedicated member of a community of faith makes you part of something important, something bigger than yourself, something that, quite literally, can be life-changing."

"So you are saying the whole thing is relational. Relationship with God and with other Christians."

"Yes. And as in all relationships, what you get out of it depends on what you put into it."

"I understand. I have a friend whose family is rich. Lots of people in school wanted to be her friend just because she was rich, and they thought there might be something there for them. They didn't really care about her; they were just interested because she was rich. It was really kind of sad."

"I think that's a pretty good analogy. Some people *go to church* with no thought of honoring and loving God, but looking to get something from him. He's already died for them, and offered to save them, but that doesn't seem to be enough. They want something else. They want God to make everything nice in their lives. They think of God as if he were Santa Claus. They have a wish list, and they want stuff from him. But relationships don't work like that."

"Never thought of it like that before," Diane said, and sipped her coffee. "I'm gonna need to think about this some more."

"Thinking is always a good thing to do," I said.

There was a brief pause and Conner said, "I didn't have breakfast, and I'm hungry. I'm gonna go get a scone. Anybody want anything?"

"No, thanks," Diane said.

I said I was good.

As Conner headed up to the counter to get a scone, Diane said, "Okay, I see what you're saying about relationship and all, you know, with God and with other Christians, but I still have questions about the roll of organized religion in the world. It just doesn't seem relevant anymore. What about that?"

"Well, I think that depends on how you understand relevance. A thing may, in fact, be extremely relevant, but if a given individual does not see or understand its relevance, for that person that thing appears to be irrelevant when in fact it is not."

"So organized religion is relevant whether people think so or not?"

"I can't say that all organized religion is relevant. I can only say that the Christian church is relevant whether people think so or not."

"So you're saying only Christianity is relevant? It's the only true religion?"

"In my view."

"Wow. That's kind of narrow, isn't it?"

"Depends on whether or not you believe the Bible to be God's communication to humankind."

Diane's eyes narrowed a little as she considered what I'd said.

"But going down the road," I said, "of which religions are or are not acceptable to God takes us in a very different direction. Your question is about the relevance of organized religion. As long as you understand that what I say has to do with the relevance of Christianity, I think that is still the conversation we need to have right now. The other one we can have some other time."

She shrugged. "Okay. Sure. So, how is the Christian church relevant?"

"God exists," I said. "Moral absolutes exist. Right and wrong exist. Humans do wrong things. They sin by violating God's laws. This is true of all people. Therefore, all people need to be saved. They need to be forgiven by God. He offers forgiveness to all who come to him through faith in Jesus. The church is responsible for spreading that message and helping people come to know God so they can enjoy a relationship with him. That makes the church relevant."

"But if someone doesn't think they need to be saved …"

"Because they are mistaken about their sinfulness and their need to be saved doesn't mean the church is irrelevant. It means they are mistaken."

"Doesn't it mean that organized religion is irrelevant to them?"

"As in, *what's relevant to you may not be relevant to me?*"

"Yes."

"That only works if you embrace the idea that there is no objective reality, no objective truth. It only works if you embrace the idea that all things are absolutely relative or personally subjective. In which case you can speak of my truth, your truth, his truth, her truth, but you can never refer to *the* truth. Nothing is ultimately true, therefore, nothing is ultimately relevant. Relevant is whatever a person decides is relevant."

"I see what you are saying, but isn't it true that if a thing isn't relevant to me, it's not relevant to me? I mean if I'm not interested in reading mystery novels then I'm not interested in reading mystery novels. End of discussion. I'm not interested in it. It's my preference."

"Some things are like that, yes. Personal preference is like personal opinion. I like pepperoni pizza; I don't like mushroom pizza. Simple as that. But not everything is a matter of preference or opinion. I may prefer that the sun not come up tomorrow. Sun is probably going to come up tomorrow whether I prefer it to or not."

"Okay. So you're saying that some things are the case, and personal preference or opinion do not matter because things are the way they are. And you're saying that that applies to relevance."

"To the church being relevant," I said.

Diane sipped some more of her coffee and said, "And so organized religion, you're saying, is relevant because God exists, moral absolutes exist, sin exists, people need to be saved from sin, and it is the church's job to get that message out. Therefore, the church is relevant whether people think it is or not."

"Nicely put. Yes, that's what I'm saying."

"But is the church doing what it is supposed to do?"

"Some of them are; some of them are not."

"So, could we say that some churches, the ones that are doing what they are supposed to do, are relevant, and the ones that are not, are not relevant?"

"I think it may be fair to say that."

"So some churches are relevant and some are not."

"Some churches are spiritually dead. They just don't realize it."

"Zombie churches," Diane said.

I smiled. "I guess you could say that."

"Be good to avoid those churches."

"Find one that is making a difference in people's lives and join in."

Diane nodded, thought for a moment, and said, "But is organized religion really making any positive contribution in the world?"

"It is. Lots of positive stuff going on. Christians give over 50 billion dollars each year to charities worldwide.

That's a lot of money. And there are over 430,000 full-time missionaries serving around the world. Some run orphanages, some operate schools, some minister in churches where they teach Bible classes and help individuals they encounter. Some run youth programs of different kinds, some work in medical missions. Lives around the world are being impacted by Christians."

"That's impressive," Diane said. "You never hear about any of that."

"The media, for the most part, is not friendly toward Christianity. They are quick to cover anything negative, but the positive stuff goes unreported."

"That's a shame. If more people knew what Christianity was doing in the world, they might tend to be more interested."

"Exactly."

She considered me for a moment, then said, "You really think there is a concerted effort to minimize Christianity?"

"I do."

"Why would anyone want to minimize something making a positive difference?"

"Because while the church does a great deal of good in the world, it also condemns certain behaviors and lifestyles as unacceptable to God. Many of the people in media are unhappy about that."

"So, you think they intentionally ignore the good stuff the church is doing in the world."

"How would you explain their lack of coverage of the good being done?" I asked.

She shook her head and said, "I don't know. But what I do know is that I'm glad Conner suggested that I talk with you, and I'm glad I came. This has been very helpful. I still need to think about things, and I need to look around at some different churches and see if there's a good one around where I can see if I fit in."

"There are plenty of them," I said.

"I assume that you go to a church that is making a difference."

"I do."

"Which one?"

I told her, and she made a note of it in her phone. Conner was all smiles as they headed for the door. As they left, I said a silent prayer for Diane, asking God to help her find the right church for her.

Chapter 8
Ed and the Church's Role in Politics

"Hey, Dr. Baker," Conner said. "How are you today?"

"I'm good. How about you?"

"Not bad. This is my friend, Ed."

I stood and offered my hand.

"He has some questions about the church and politics."

Ed was a little guy—five foot six maybe, and skinny. He had a long, scraggly beard that reached halfway down his chest. He wore baggy jeans and a tee shirt that said, "*The fool has said in his heart, there is no God. Psalm 14:1.*" And though he looked to be in his mid-twenties, he was already losing his hair. We shook hands. "Nice to meet you, Ed."

"Nice to meet you."

We all sat down, and I said, "So, the church and politics. What is it you are concerned about?"

"I think Christians should be socially and politically engaged, trying to make American society a better place to live. And I think being involved in politics is one way to do it. But I have some friends who say that Christians should not be involved in politics. This guy I know, Sean, says politics is worldly, whatever that means, and so corrupt that a Christian cannot be involved. I think he's wrong, but I don't know how to prove it."

"*Proving* your point," I said, "might be difficult because I suspect this question is mostly a matter of opinion. But we can certainly provide some arguments that might convince your friend to rethink his position."

"I'll take anything you've got."

"We can start with the idea that being involved in politics is worldly. While the New Testament does condemn *worldliness*, the idea is being devoid of spirituality. In other words, being a person not interested in spiritual concerns, living life without interest in God and right living. A worldly person is one who is only really interested in physical pleasures and pursuits. To identify a thing as worldly and therefore unacceptable for a Christian, unless that behavior is condemned in Scripture, betrays a misunderstanding and a misuse of the concept."

"Conner said you used to be a professor."

"Yes."

Ed nodded to himself as if I had somehow confirmed a suspicion. Then he said, "Maybe you can give me an example."

"Sure. The New Testament condemns participation in an orgy. So one could identify the participation in an orgy as being a worldly practice that Christians ought to avoid. But to simply use the words worldly or worldliness willy nilly to identify things of which one does not approve is inappropriate."

"And since the Bible does not condemn participation in politics," Ed said, "you can't call it a worldly practice that Christians need to avoid."

"Exactly."

Ed sipped his coffee. "Okay, that addresses the worldliness issue, but is that going to be enough to change Sean's mind?"

"Probably not."

"So what else can I say to him?"

"A logical argument might be effective."

"A logical argument."

"Try reasoning with him."

"I thought I had already done that."

"What argument did you use?"

"I told him that Christians ought to do whatever they can to make society a better place."

"And his response was …?

"He said that didn't include engaging in worldly behavior."

I smiled. "Yeah, a lot of people who are not trained in critical analysis and designing sound arguments reason that way."

"I'm not sure I'm following you."

"I'm assuming his argument goes something like this: Participating in worldly things is wrong. Politics is a worldly pursuit. Therefore, participating in politics is wrong."

"Yeah, that's pretty much what he's arguing."

"Well, it is clear that he does not understand how the idea of worldliness is to be understood. It can't mean anything not directly spiritual, because most of life's activities would then be classified as worldly and, therefore, not be appropriate Christian behavior: eating, sleeping, putting gas in your car, washing your clothes, and a thousand other things. That's obviously not how the idea of worldliness in the New Testament is to be understood. You have to make that point and not let him sidestep it. Hold his feet to the fire. Worldliness doesn't mean just whatever he decides it means."

"Okay, what else?"

Ed wanted to move things right along.

"Well," I said, "I would argue that a huge part of Christianity involves helping people: doing what one can to relieve suffering. In the New Testament, Jesus talked about giving a cup of cold water in his name. He healed people both physically and spiritually. He taught them how to live better and how to be better people. All that contains a social element. The presence of Christians in society, doing the kinds of things that ease the burdens people carry, make society a better place. Sometimes to make society a better place, you have to engage in the political process: get money budgeted for social concerns, get laws passed that make society more fair for everyone involved."

"That's the argument I tried to make," Ed said.

"And?"

"And he said that in the Bible there's no record of Christians being involved in politics. He said doing good was supposed to be done individually, one person interacting with another person."

"It is true that in the New Testament there is no record of direct involvement by Christians in politics.

However, one reason for that had to do with the sociopolitical context. Political activity was not an option for the average person in the first century. They didn't engage in politics because they couldn't. The world they lived in didn't allow for it. That is not the case, however, in America. We can be involved. And, I believe, we should be impacting the political process as much as possible to make it a better process, to make America a better place."

"What about the idea that the political process is corrupt?"

"I suspect your friend's concern is that if the Christian puts him or herself in a corrupt context, he or she might be corrupted."

"Yes."

"But isn't that always the case? Isn't society in general a pretty corrupt place? Isn't there lots of bad stuff going on that Christians ought to avoid?"

"I guess so. Like what?"

"Like what. Well, suppose you work for a company where some of the sales people lie about the product they're selling, saying that it is one hundred percent made in America. But actually it is only assembled in America. The parts are made in China. Because some of the sales staff lie about the product, does that mean you are lying about the product?"

"No."

"That's correct. You can work for a company where some of the people lie, or steal, or cheat, without you becoming a liar, or a thief, and a cheater."

"And so even if some politicians or political processes are dishonest," Ed said, "me being involved doesn't make me dishonest."

"Right."

"So there's no reason Christians shouldn't be involved in the political process."

"Not only is there no reason they shouldn't be," I said, "but there are plenty of reasons they should be, both formally and informally and at different levels."

"Formally and informally?"

"Sure. They can hold an elected office, that would be formally, or they can be involved as a citizen, which would be informal involvement."

"So, one way or the other," Ed said, "Christians ought to be doing something to make society a better place to live."

"Yes."

"Like what?"

"What should they be doing, or what should they be trying to accomplish?"

"Let's start with what they should be trying to accomplish."

"Well, they should be trying to address moral issues such as abortion. And obviously they should be concerned about social justice issues, making sure society is fair and just for everyone. They should be involved in trying to help those who really need help. There's lots of stuff Christians ought to be concerned about."

"So, one way," Ed said, "to make a difference in how things are is to run for office and then try to get laws passed and programs funded that will make a difference."

"That would be one way."

"But as a percentage of the entire Christian population of the U.S.," Ed said, "those who could or world run for office is very small."

"It is."

"So, the other option is informal involvement."

"Yes."

"What kind of things can Christians do to make a difference?" Ed asked.

"For one, they can vote for the candidate that stands for the ideology and values they have. They can vote across party lines if necessary to get the right person elected."

"The right person being the one who shares their perspective."

"Sure."

"Okay, so, voting. What else?"

"They can write, which today means email, elected officials at both the state and federal levels and tell them what they want, what they are interested in, and how they want their representative to vote on a given concern. Elected officials need to know what their constituents believe and want. The only way for elected officials to know is for us to tell them."

Ed nodded and drank some of his coffee. Then he said, "Voting, communicating. What else?"

"They should attend local party meetings, and volunteer to help get things done."

"What kind of things?"

"Well, like collecting signatures to get irresponsible politicians recalled and replaced, or to get enough signatures on a proposed bill or program to submit it for consideration."

Ed was nodding again, holding his cup of coffee in both hands up near his mouth, ready to take another drink. But he was thinking, not drinking. When he had apparently thought enough, he took another drink of his coffee. I waited. After a couple of swallows of coffee, Ed said, "You mentioned moral issues like abortion, and social justice issues. Can you talk about what you mean by social justice?"

"Well, there's the obvious stuff, like kids who have no family and who are on their own. They need help. Some kids can't read or do math. They need after-school tutoring programs. The homeless need places to sleep and a hot meal to eat. Those sorts of things are kind of obvious."

"What are the things that are not so obvious?" Ed asked.

"Well, I think Christians ought to be concerned and work toward insuring basic rights like free speech, freedom of religion, the right to keep and bear arms, those sorts of things."

"Really?"

"Really. Christians often think that they ought to focus their attention on things that appear to me more directly related to the Christian mission, different forms of Christian outreach. But without securing our basic rights, everything else is in jeopardy."

"I hadn't thought of it that way," Ed said.

"Most people don't. But if our right to free speech is diminished by censorship of various kinds, how will we share the good news of Jesus? If our right to gather for worship and otherwise practice the tenents of our faith is diminished, how do we go about doing what God expects us to do?"

"And that's a right?"

"The freedom of religion clause of the First Amendment says, '*Congress shall make no law respecting an establishment of religion, or prohibiting the free exercise thereof* ...' The most important part of that is the second part of the clause ... '*or the free exercise thereof.*' The right includes not just the right to believe what you want to believe, but the absolute right to practice it, to put your faith into action and do what you believe God wants you to do. The *free exercise thereof.* And there are people in our society right now who are trying to minimize the role of religion in society, telling people of faith that religion is something to be practiced only in the privacy of their own home. But that was not what the founders had in mind. Christians need to fight for their rights, or soon they will have not rights."

"Wow. I didn't realize."

"Because you are a self-determined being," I said, "freedom, as much as you can possibly have, is an absolute necessity if you are to be happy and healthy, able to excel and achieve, living up to the potential God put in each of us. Beyond all else, Christians need to fight to secure our fundamental rights."

"What you're saying is startling. This is important stuff. Why don't more churches encourage their members to be more involved in sociopolitical concerns?"

I took a drink of my coffee. "Because most of them are worried about offending people and losing some of their members, which impacts the collection plate."

"Money? You're saying it comes down to money?"

"Unfortunately, yes. Suppose you have a membership of 300. Suppose 75% of them are republican, and 25%

democrat. Most of the members are conservative. But 25% will be more progressive. If you offend them, and they leave your church, you lose 25% of your income. What would happen to you if you lost 25% of your personal income?"

Ed did a quick calculation. "I'd have to decide on being able to put gas in my car, having insurance on my car, or eating."

"Exactly. It's similar for churches. There are expenses to be paid. Got to have an income. If you annoy people by advocating ideas they don't embrace, you diminish your income."

"That's really sad. Christianity ought to be above that. It should be about doing what's right, not about keeping people happy."

"I agree. But we don't live in an ideal world; we live in a real world where things are not always as they should be."

"So what do we do? Just leave it alone?"

"No, I would not suggest that. I would encourage church leaders to try to raise the level of their members' political awareness and try to convert the liberals."

"Bring them out of the darkness of left wing thinking into the light of conservatism," Ed said.

I smiled. "Something like that."

Ed drained the rest of the coffee from his cup and said, "This has been really interesting and helpful, Dr. Baker. Thank you."

"Glad to help."

"If I have more questions, can I come back?"

"Of course."

Conner was smiling as they left. He was always happy when I could help one of his friends.

Chapter 9
Candice and Abortion

Candice had short red hair, fair skin, freckles, green eyes, and looked as unhappy a person as I had seen in a long time. Conner had introduced her and said, "Candice has some questions she needs help with. I told her you used to be a philosophy professor, but before that a minister."

Candice jumped right in. "He said you really helped him with a problem he had, and he was sure you could help me."

"Well," I said, "I hope I measure up to Conner's confidence."

"I'm pregnant," she said. "And my boyfriend wants me to get an abortion. He says we're not ready to have a baby yet."

Apparently Candice figured that was enough for me to go with, so I said, "And how do you feel about that?"

"I don't want to get an abortion, but he's kind of insisting. My friends say I should get one if I want to, and my parents say I shouldn't."

"Why don't you want to get an abortion?"

"Because I feel like I would be killing my baby. Don … that's my boyfriend, he says there is no baby, that there's only a clump of cells. But I believe there is a baby. Am I wrong?"

"No, you're not wrong."

"How can I make him understand? I love him, and I want to be with him. But I don't want to kill my baby. But I don't know how to convince him."

"Are you familiar with any of the history of abortion in America?"

"No. What would that have to do with anything?"

"To understand how we got to where we are today in relation to abortion being right or wrong, you need to understand how abortion got to be legal in America."

"You mean it wasn't always legal?"

"No, it wasn't. In fact there was a time when nearly all Americans considered abortion to be murder."

"Murder?"

"When someone intentionally kills a person who has done nothing wrong, what do we call that?"

She thought for a moment. "Murder?"

"That's how most people thought of abortion until the feminist movement began to campaign to have it legalized."

"The feminist movement."

"The feminist movement had some really good things to say and made some good and important differences for women in America. I consider myself a feminist in that I believe that women are equal to men and must be treated accordingly, and must receive equal pay for equal work.

111

Those sorts of things. But the more radical version of the feminist movement has embraced some questionable ideas that, I think, are problematic."

"And abortion is one of those?"

"Yes."

"Why do you think abortion is wrong?"

"That is the question, isn't it? And to answer it, we need to understand the history of how things came about."

Candice shrugged and said, "Okay. If it will help me understand so I can convince Don."

"Once you know the history and the arguments, you'll be able to explain it to Don. Whether or not he will be convinced and agree with you is another matter."

That thought, apparently, hadn't occurred to her, and she seemed disappointed. But then she said, "Yeah, I guess that's right. But maybe if I can explain it to him, he'll see why I can't kill my baby."

"If he loves you, he'll honor your decision."

"I hope," she said. "Okay, so tell me about the history of abortion in America."

"The Supreme Court legalized abortion in 1973. Before then, some states allowed abortion, some allowed it in some circumstances, but thirty states prohibited it in all circumstances."

"I didn't know that."

"Most younger people don't. They grew up with it being legal and just assume it has always been legal. But it was only legal in some places. In fact, only one state, New York allowed abortion in general."

"So, what happened to change all that?"

"A case came before the Supreme Court, Roe v Wade, and they ruled that a woman had the right to choose to have an abortion. But the interesting thing in all that is how public opinion had changed so that the Supreme Court, that is supposed to make decisions based on law not on public opinion, decided it was prudent to bow to public opinion and ruled in favor of abortion."

"Is that really what happened?"

"You might be surprised at how many legal experts think so."

She sipped her coffee, thought for a moment, and said, "So, what happened to change public opinion?"

"When the pro-abortion people first began their campaign to get abortion legalized, nearly everyone in the country understood the issue to be one of legalizing the killing of yet to be born babies. In other words, most people understood abortion to be killing an unborn baby. And nearly everyone was opposed to the idea of killing unborn babies. The pro-abortion people realized that as long as that was the issue, they were not going to get abortion legalized. The people were simply not going to agree that killing unborn babies was a good idea."

"I can't imagine anyone in her right mind would think it is a good idea."

"Yeah, well, some did. But they understood that they were fighting an uphill battle and were probably going to lose. Someone, however, realized that if they could change the focus of the discussion, they might have a chance. And it occurred to someone that since the women's movement was about women's rights, they could make the abortion issue about a woman's right to choose. So they made the debate about a woman having the right to choose what to do with her own body. It's her body they argued. She has the right to decide what to do regarding her own body. And given the momentum the feminist movement had, and the number of people who were in favor of women's rights, and all the grief millions of angry women could give the men in the country if they didn't get what they wanted, who was going to say that a woman didn't have the right to decide what to do with her own body?"

"That's a very good point," Candice said. "Why shouldn't a woman have the right to decide what to do when it comes to her own body?"

"Exactly. And if it was just her body, then I can't imagine there would be a problem. But because we're talking about abortion, it is not just the woman's body that is involved. There is also a baby. What about the baby's body?"

Tears welled up in Candice's eyes. "I'm sorry," she said, dabbing at her eyes with a napkin. "There is a baby's body, isn't there?"

"There is," I said. "That's what the entire question is about. A baby, once conceived, is living and growing inside the mother's body. It is a separate being, with a body and an identity of its own. The question is, can the mother decide to end its life so she doesn't have to carry the baby to term and give birth?"

Candice said, "And the pro-abortion people said, no, she shouldn't have to do that. She should be able to kill the baby if she wants to."

"That's right. But the pro-abortion people were smart, and they realized that even if they changed the focus of the

114

debate from killing an unborn baby to a woman's right to choose, people could still argue that the whole issue was still about killing unborn babies. Lots of people were misdirected by the right to choose argument, but enough were still focused on the real issue that pro-abortionists were having trouble bringing people over to their side. So what they decided to do was say that there is no baby."

"No baby?"

"That's right."

"How could they say there is no baby? I mean that's the whole point. There's a baby in there. And it's growing and it's gonna be born. How can you say there is no baby? I don't understand that. That's what Don is saying—that there's no baby to kill. But how can that be?"

"Their argument is that the baby is not a person until much later in the pregnancy. Some say it is not a person until it is born. They got some liberal doctors to say that in the early stages of pregnancy, all there is is a clump of cells, a gob of uterine goo as it were, and that there is no identifiable person there. Since there is no person present, but only a clump of cells, you cannot be killing a yet to be born baby."

"Is that right?"

"Got your phone with you?"

"Sure." She took it out of her back pocket.

"Do a search for images of an eight week old fetus."

She did. "That's what an eight week old fetus looks like?"

"It is."

"It's clearly a baby."

"It is. Sixty-six percent of the legal abortions performed are performed within the first eight weeks; ninety-two percent are performed within the first thirteen weeks."

"So, if a fetus looks like this at eight weeks, what does it look like at thirteen weeks?"

"Look it up."

She did. "Oh my goodness. How could anyone say that is not a baby?"

"As evocative as those images are," I said, "I think there is an even more compelling argument."

"I don't see what could be more compelling than this," Candice said.

"Think about it from this point of view. When two human beings reproduce, what is it that they reproduce?"

"I'm not sure what you mean."

"Well, when two humans reproduce, do they reproduce a thing that is categorized as a swine?"

"You mean a pig?"

"Yes."

"No. People don't reproduce pigs."

"How about something that is categorized as feline?"

"No."

"Canine?"

"No."

"Equine?"

"No."

"Bovine?"

"No."

"Okay, so humans don't reproduce swine, feline, canine, equine, bovine, and so forth. What do they reproduce?"

"Humans reproduce humans."

"Yes. When two humans reproduce, that which they reproduce is human."

"Of course."

"Do they reproduce something that is non-human?"

"No."

"Can they?"

"I don't think so."

"I don't, either. They can't reproduce something that is not human but will become a human. Humans don't reproduce non-humans."

She considered me for a moment. "I agree."

"What we seem to be saying is that when two humans reproduce, that which they reproduce is also human."

"Yes."

"Is it alive?"

"Is it alive? Certainly it's alive. And it is growing."

"That's right. That's what pregnancy is about. When a baby is conceived, it is a living, growing human being. It may not be able to do all the things a mature human can do, but neither can a newborn infant. Yet we acknowledge that the newborn infant is a person, and as such, has rights, the chief right being the right to life."

"Yes."

"So a fetus is not a non-person, not a non-human, not a glob of cells that is nothing specific and has, therefore, no rights. It is a living, growing, developing human being that belongs to the family of beings called humans, and as such has rights."

"Yes," she said almost triumphantly. "My baby is a human being. A living, growing, developing human being. And I won't kill it."

"You think you'll be able to convince Don?"

She thought about it. "I don't know. But either way, I'm not going to kill my baby."

She sat back in her chair and thought, sipping some of her coffee as she did.

I looked at Conner. It was clear that he felt for her. She was in a tough spot. She might have to choose between the man she loved and her baby.

After a long moment, Candice said, "If he loves me, he'll understand and accept my decision."

"And if he doesn't?" I asked.

"Then he and I both have to live with it."

She drank some more of her coffee, and appeared to have made peace with her situation. Then she said, "I have another question."

I nodded.

"Some of my friends will say to me, *It's your decision. You do what you think you must do.* And what they'll mean is that if I choose not to have an abortion, that's my decision, but if someone else chooses to have an abortion, well that's her decision. Either way, it is the woman's choice."

I nodded again. "That's what most people would say."

"But if what you are saying is true, how can it be right for any woman to decide to kill her baby, to kill a living, developing human being who's done nothing wrong?"

"Good question," I said. "The idea that it is a woman's right to decide what to do has been pounded into our collective consciousness to the point that most people don't see the inherent contradiction involved in the idea of abortion. If there's a baby present, it is not just her body involved, and she cannot, therefore, simply choose to kill another person, even if that person is living inside her for a while."

"So, if that's the case, and, I mean logically how can anyone deny it, if there's a baby present, and of course there is, that's what being pregnant is about, then how can it be legal to kill another human being? How can people be so foolish?"

"Narcissism," I said.

"Narcissism."

"An unparalleled level of self-absorption."

"I'm not sure I'm following you."

"Selfishness," I said. "Unless there is an additional medical problem involved, and usually there isn't, a woman wants an abortion because she doesn't want to have a baby. All she's thinking about is herself. I'm not ready to be a mother. I don't want to have a baby. I, I, I. It's all about her. She's not thinking about the baby growing inside of her, not thinking about the life she is about to terminate, not thinking about the child at all; she's only thinking about herself. She's completely self-absorbed. Maybe it's because she's too young, or too old, or because she has no husband or anyone to help her, or because of the financial burden. But whatever the reason, all she's thinking about is herself. And that is entirely inappropriate."

"I see what you are saying. It's not very complimentary, but I think you're right. And just because it is going to be difficult for her, does that mean she has the right to kill the baby?"

"And the simplest solution is to say that there is no baby."

"But there is," Candice said. "And we all know there is. So that whole argument is just silly. So why doesn't the government do something about it? Why don't they make it illegal, like it used to be?"

"Because over half the country would be up in arms if they did."

"Doesn't make it right. The government is supposed to protect the people's rights. What about the rights of the baby? It has a right to live. The least she could do is put it up for adoption."

"I agree."

"What can we do about it?" Candice asked.

"Write your congressman. Start a campaign about the rights of the yet to be born. Collect signatures. Try to get the law changed."

"If Don won't go along with me and won't marry me and help me raise our baby, I won't have the time to take on a project like that."

"Most people don't."

"So what happens?"

"We talk about it when we can. We try to teach people. Try to change their minds. In time, people may begin to think differently about the rights of the yet to be born."

She nodded as she thought about all of it, her eyes roaming over the surface of the table between us as she did.

"Well," she said, looking at Connor, "you were right. He gave me a good answer. Thanks for suggesting this." Then, to me she said, "Thank you, Dr. Baker. This has been very helpful."

"My pleasure," I said. "I hope things work out for you. I'll pray that they do."

Chapter 10
Bill and Sexual Orientation Issues

Conner was getting himself and Bill some coffee. I still had most of my large light roast with two creams. Conner had introduced Bill, as he introduced most of the people he brought to talk with me, as a friend. Bill had added that they'd gone through high school together. Bill was studying ministry at one of the three Christian universities in town and was having trouble with what he described as a ministry issue and a personal concern.

"Sexual orientation," Bill said as Conner was returning with their coffee.

"What about it?" I asked.

"Well, from a ministry point of view, I'm having trouble figuring out how I'm going to deal with it."

"And none of your professors can help you with it?"

"They don't consider it a problem. Near as I can figure, most academics, even the Christian ones, have accepted the idea that non-hetero orientations are fine."

"Non-hetero?"

"Short for non-heterosexual. There are so many different kinds of sexual orientations and ways of identifying, instead of trying to refer to them individually it's easier to refer to them all as non-heterosexual. I just shorten it non-hetero or non-het."

"I see. So, most of your professors don't see a problem with non-hetero orientations, but you do."

"Honestly, at this point I don't know what to think. I mean, I know what the Bible says about it. I've read all the texts and studied all the Hebrew and Greek words. And I know the argument that the anti-homosexual perspective in the Bible is just an ancient homophobic cultural construct. I understand all that. But when the Bible says one thing and the pro-homosexual advocates assert something else … well, I'm just having difficulty working it all out in my mind."

"And you're worried about how to respond to the question when it comes up in local ministry."

"Yeah."

"You also mentioned a personal facet to the concern."

"Yeah. It's tearing my family apart."

"A sexual orientation concern?"

"Yes. My little brother just recently told my parents and me that he's what he referred to as a genderqueer."

"Genderqueer," I said.

"Yeah. I looked it up. Supposedly it is someone who doesn't identify with traditional gender identifications, but who sees himself or herself as neither or both genders at the same time. I'm not sure how one can be neither male nor female. But Michael says he's both male and female, but he's leaning toward female as a presentation self. That's what he called it, a presentation self."

"And that wasn't well-received?"

"My family is very conservative."

I nodded and sipped my coffee.

"He says he intends from now on to be Michele. He's going to grow his hair long and get breast implants. He's going to be a female on top but remain a male on the bottom."

"Who's he going to have sex with," I asked, "males, females, or both?"

Bill shook his head. "I couldn't bring myself to ask."

"I see. And you want me to help you figure out how to respond to ..."

"Michele, he says. But he'll always be Michael to me."

"How do you feel like responding?"

"I love him. He's my brother. But he's my brother, not my sister, or my sister-brother, or whatever he thinks he'll be after buying himself a pair of boobs, some makeup, and a new wardrobe."

I nodded and looked for a moment into my coffee cup.

"Look," Bill said. "I know how this must sound, but I'm not trying to be hateful or sarcastic or anything. I love my brother. And my parents. And they're heartbroken right now. And so am I. I really need help in trying to understand this. But I also love God and want to serve him. And if he says homosexuality or whatever this is is wrong, then ..." He held out his hands palms up and shrugged.

"I understand," I said. "You're between a rock and a hard place."

"A very big rock and a very hard place."

"So, what is it you'd like me to do?"

"Well, I already know what the Bible says about homosexuality … assuming this thing with Michael fits under that general heading. I don't know. I guess what I'm not sure about is whether or not the whole thing about the evils of homosexuality is just an ancient cultural construct like some people say, or if God really disapproves of orientations other than heterosexual. And if he does, then so do I."

"Okay, I understand where you're coming from. What God thinks is very important to me as well. But let me ask you, if you were a minister in a local church and became aware that a man in your church was having an affair with his secretary, would you confront him and demand that he stop or leave your church?

"No. I wouldn't handle it that way."

"Why not?"

"Because you just don't issue an ultimatum that ends up driving people away."

"Why not?"

"Because Jesus came to save people, not to condemn them."

"Right. So, what would you do?"

"I'd talk with him and try to help him see that what he was doing was wrong and hurtful and that he needed to stop."

"So you'd try to help."

"Yes."

"What if he told you it was no use, that he loved this other woman and was going to divorce his wife and marry his secretary?"

"Well, then we'd have to talk about it some more, assuming that he'd talk with me, and I'd try to get him to break it off with his mistress and reconcile with his wife."

"Okay. But what you wouldn't do is tell him he wasn't welcome at your church."

"No, I wouldn't do that."

"Why not?"

Bill said, "You've asked me that a couple of times now. "I'm not sure what you're looking for."

"What is the church?" I asked.

"The body of Christ."

"Made up of whom?"

"Saved people."

"Saved from what?"

"Their sins."

"So they don't sin any more?"

What I was getting at suddenly dawned on him. "The church is made up of imperfect people who continue to struggle with sin. It is an ongoing problem."

I nodded and sipped my coffee. "What if you found out that a guy who was an accountant at a large firm was cooking the books and stealing money from them?"

"Same thing. I'd try to help him see that his behavior was not only wrong but destructive, and try to help him stop."

"And you wouldn't tell him he wasn't welcome at your church."

"No."

"Okay, so can we say, then, that if it is the case that God feels that sexual orientations and gender identities other than heterosexuality are unacceptable to him, we would treat non-heteros with as much kindness and love as we would anyone else caught up in sinful behavior?"

"Sure," Bill said. "All people are sinful. You, me, everybody. There are no degrees of sin. Non-heterosexuality is no worse than any other sin."

"Okay. So, then, as far as your brother is concerned, even though you are concerned about his, what shall we call them, his sexual challenges, like you said, he is still your brother, and you love him."

"Yes."

"So you continue to love him even though you might be disappointed by his behavior."

"That goes without saying. What I'm more concerned about is the moral aspect, whether what he is doing is moral or not. What does God think about what he's doing?"

"Okay, let's get to that. Clearly, the Bible says homosexuality, and by extension all other forms of non-heterosexual behavior, are immoral."

"Right."

"However, some claim that the biblical condemnation of non-heterosexual behavior grows out of an ancient cultural construct rooted in ignorance. If they had known then what we know now, ancient people would not have disapproved."

"Yeah," Bill said. "How do we know that is not the case?"

"Well, first, making that claim suggests that the biblical condemnation grows out of a human cultural construct rather than out of God's disapproval. In other words, to say that the Bible's condemnation of homosexuality is cultural is to deny that God was expressing his disapproval of the behavior. But here's the thing, if God disapproves, it is not a matter of it being a cultural construct. It is a matter of divine judgment. Ancient people are not saying the behavior is unacceptable, God is saying it. And that's a very different matter, is it not?"

"Never thought of it like that before," Bill said. "But isn't the case that the message of the Bible was impacted by the culture of the writers?"

"That is the case. But we must engage in a very rigorous process to determine which parts are attributed to culture and which parts are supracultural."

"Supracultural?"

"Above culture," I said. "In other words, the parts that you can't simply toss out, saying that the practice, the behavior, the condemnation, whatever, was associated with the culture of that time and place."

"So, you're saying it is not easy to figure out what was culture and what was God's will."

"Exactly."

"Okay, so how do we figure out whether what the Bible says about homosexuality is rooted in human culture or God's judgment?"

"I think you have to begin with the assumption that if God created human beings, he created them the way he wanted them to be: which is male and female, with very specific male and female sex and reproductive organs designed for the propagation of the species."

"So, you're saying that since God designed male and female for the propagation of the species, males and females should get together and make babies."

"Yes."

"But as long as there is plenty of heterosexual propagation going on, what would be wrong with non-hetero activity as well?"

"Well, let's say I designed the baseball bat, and I designed it to hit baseballs in a fun sport called baseball. If someone plays baseball and hits baseballs with the bat, what is the harm if he then also goes around breaking windows with it? Or bashing mailboxes with it? Or uses it in any other destructive ways? Can I, as the designer of the baseball bat, say, *But that's not what I designed it for. You are misusing what I designed and created.*"

"In that analogy," Bill said, "I get what you're saying, but I don't think that piece of logic is going to convince anyone of anything."

"Maybe not. But it is a place to begin. If God designed sex to be used one way and some people use it another way ..."

I could see that Bill was skeptical.

"Okay," I said, "let's turn it around and come at it from a different perspective. Lay aside for a moment that people have decided that non-hetero activity is acceptable, and ask if that were not the case, if the practice were not being advocated, is there anything about the practice that suggests that non-heterosexual activity is a good and acceptable behavior for human beings?"

"What about the idea that love all by itself is a good thing?"

"Love is a good thing. But that doesn't automatically make sex with the person you love a good thing. A person loves his or her children, but doesn't have sex with them. A person loves his or her siblings, but doesn't have sex with them. A person can love someone of the same sex, like best friends. That doesn't mean they should have sex with each other."

Bill was thinking.

"If people weren't advocating non-hetero activity, can you think of anything to recommend it?"

"What if a person is just not interested in the opposite sex?"

"First, answer my question."

"All right. No. I can't think of anything to recommend it. But now you answer mine. What if a person is just not interest in the opposite sex?"

"That's a good question. Sexual impulses are very strong. Where do they come from?"

"Well, if I remember my freshman biology correctly, sexual impulses come from sex hormones—testosterone, estrogen, those sorts of things."

"Basically, yes."

"But what if a guy, for instance, has too much estrogen in his system?"

"Well, then things are not working the way things are supposed to work."

"Wouldn't something like that be beyond the control of the individual?"

"The impulses, yes. The acting on them, no."

"What do you mean?"

"Are there some people who have very strong impulses to have sex with children?"

"There must be. Otherwise, there wouldn't be so much child porn."

"I agree. What do we say to people with impulses to have sex with children?"

"That they can't."

"That's right."

"Yeah, but that doesn't involve consenting adults."

"True. But that's not exactly the question we're discussing. In discussing impulses, we're asking if impulses must be acted on."

"And you're saying they don't?"

"What if someone has a defective MAOA gene? That's the gene that regulates aggression. If someone has a defective MAOA gene, they have very strong impulses to be aggressive and violent. Do we simply say, well, they have very strong impulses toward aggression and violence but can't help it, so just let them be violent?"

"No. But they might be hurting other people. Non-hetero activity doesn't hurt anyone."

"How do you know that?" I asked. "How do you know that in the long run non-heterosexual behavior is not harmful?"

"Are you saying it is?"

"No. I don't know that it is. How do you know it isn't?"

Bill considered me for a long moment and drank some of his coffee.

"The point is," I said, "that we do not know it isn't harmful, so we cannot argue that no one is being hurt. Maybe

131

there are long range negative effects, and we do not know it."

"But maybe there aren't."

"That's right. We do not have enough information to argue that point either way."

"So, your comment about the MAOA gene is wrong."

"No."

"Why not?"

"Because the point wasn't that people are being hurt. The point was that just because someone has strong impulses that are beyond their control, we do not simply allow their behavior."

"So, you're saying that people with a non-heterosexual orientation or identity should control their impulses."

"I'm saying that that's what we tell other people when they raise the impulses issue."

"So the impulses argument," Bill said, "I have these strong impulses … is not a good argument in favor of accepting non-heterosexual behavior."

"Part of growing up is learning to control your impulses."

"Okay, I see what you're saying, but that's not going to be enough to convince anyone."

"I agree," I said. "It is only one piece of the puzzle."

"So, what else have you got?"

"Well, a non-heterosexual orientation is certainly not normal."

"Not normal?"

"The LGBTQ community is constantly attempting to convince the rest of the world that a huge percentage of the world population is not heterosexual. The evidence, however, from which they draw their conclusion is less than convincing, consisting of so-called self-reporting that then requires speculation regarding estimates about the whole of the population. Very questionable. Multiple reliable estimates that come up with similar numbers are that 4% to 5% of the population is gay in one form or another. So, it is likely that 95% of the total human population is straight. Anything that is only 5% out of 100% does not represent the norm for the entire group. The 95% that are heterosexual represent the norm. The 5% is a deviation from the norm."

"You're saying non-heteros are deviants?"

"Statistically speaking, that which does not conform to the norm is referred to as a deviation. Heterosexuality represents the norm; non-heterosexuality does not."

Bill took in a deep breath, let it out, and sipped some more of his coffee. "Okay, look," he said, "I get what you are saying. There are all kinds of problems with trying to say a non-heterosexual orientation or identity, or whatever you call it, is perfectly acceptable. It isn't the way human sexuality is supposed to work. But none of that is helping me figure out how to deal with my brother. Why is he like this? What happened to him?"

"I don't know. No one knows, really. Science can't explain it yet. Maybe they won't ever be able to."

"I thought they'd already figured it out."

"The people who advocate non-heterosexuality claim they have the answer—that it is genetic and beyond anyone's control. But that is simply not true. People used to say there was a gay gene that made you gay. That has been debunked. There is no gay gene. Without a doubt, there are some genetic factors, sex hormones, that sort of thing. But the latest research suggests that there is no single cause. There are a number of factors that no one yet fully understands."

"How do they know there are factors other than genetics involved?"

"Identical twin studies," I said and paused, but Bill was waiting for me to go on. "As you know, identical twins are genetically identically. One egg was fertilized at conception; it divided into two zygotes, resulting in twins that have exactly the same DNA. So the genetics of one twin is the genetics of the other. Studies have been done where one of the identical twins was gay and the other one straight. If sexual orientation were only due to genetics, twins with exactly the same genetic makeup would have the same sexual orientation. But in some cases they do not. That means that there are factors other than genetics involved in the forming of sexual orientation."

"Like what?"

"Environmental factors. Sexual experiences before and during puberty, other factors."

"But my brother and I are only two and a half years apart. We grew up in the same family, the same house, we had the same experiences."

"Maybe. Maybe not. Something might have happened to Michael that you don't know about."

"Geeze. What a mess."

Bill leaned back in his chair, took another deep breath and drank some more coffee.

"Okay, so what's the bottom line here?" he asked.

"I think the bottom line for your brother and for your future ministry challenges is to stand firm in your convictions that non-heterosexual orientations, regardless of what the LBGTQ community calls them, do not represent what human sexuality is supposed to be and how it is supposed to work. But even if that is the case, Christians must understand that sexual sins are no worse than any other kind of sin, and that God expects us to be merciful to those who are struggling with sin of any kind."

"What about those who are not struggling with it? There are a bunch of them who claim that not only is it perfectly acceptable, but that it's actually preferable!"

"Yeah. That's unfortunate, isn't it? The extremists only make the situation more difficult for everyone else."

"What would you do in my place?" Bill asked.

"I'd try to be sensitive to my brother's feelings. Regardless of how he might try to pretend that he's okay with his situation, deep down inside he's got to be very unhappy. He knows what he's feeling is not normal. He knows what he's about to do is not normal. He can't feel good about that, even though there are lots of people telling him it's fine, I suspect that in his unconscious mind he knows it's not. So, I'd try to be sensitive to that. And if he and I were close, I'd try to talk with him about it. I'd encourage him to get help from a therapist who has not bought into all the LBGTQ propaganda that a non-heterosexual orientation is perfectly acceptable. Even if the impulses continue, which is likely, he can decide that he will not give in to them. He can decide to live a normal life. Lots of people do."

"So that's really what it comes down to? Impulse suppression?"

"What do people who have the impulse to have sex with children do? What do people with impulses to be violent do? What do people who have impulses to steal do? Impulse suppression is a fact of life for all people all the time. When I was still teaching, there were times when I wanted to punch a leftwing Marxist professor right in the face. But I didn't. Wouldn't have been the right thing to do. Impulse suppression."

Bill nodded as his eyes roamed over the wall behind me. "Yeah," he said. "I understand that. Just seems like there ought to be more ways to help someone than just telling them to suppress the impulse."

"Sometimes the difference between good and bad behavior comes down to nothing more than self-control."

"Yeah, I guess. Well, thank you, Dr. Baker. This has been very helpful."

"I wish I could provide a more definitive answer, but this is one of those issues where definitive left the room a long time ago."

Bill nodded and offered his hand as he stood. I stood and shook his hand, and told him I'd pray for him and for his brother, Michael. As Bill walked away, Connor said, "Thanks, Doc. No one could have helped more than you did. I appreciate it."

I nodded, and as they left I thought about how a simple thing like sex can bring such joy and at the same time such sadness.

Chapter 11
Emily and Religious Fanaticism

"Why are so many religious people so fanatical about it?" Emily asked after she and Conner sat down at my table at The Roasted Bean.

"Why is anybody fanatical about anything?" I asked.

She kept looking at me. Finally she said, "Oh, apparently that wasn't a rhetorical question."

"No," I said, "it wasn't."

"I guess because they are too invested in whatever it is they are fanatical about and don't seem to be able to moderate themselves. Their life is out of balance, and they don't realize it."

I smiled. "Or, it could be that they are simply passionate about their belief, whatever it is, and feel it is worthy of the commitment they attach to it."

"We just said the same thing. You just said it in a more positive way."

"I don't think so," I said. "The way you said it, referring to it as fanaticism, implies that serious commitment

137

to a cause or belief is problematic, a negative thing. The way I worded it allows for deep commitment without the negative connotation of the word fanatical or fanaticism."

"So you don't think religious fanaticism is a problem?"

"I think it depends on what you mean by fanaticism."

"You know what I mean: people doing crazy things in the name of religion."

"Maybe a specific example would help me focus in on what you mean."

"Islamic fanaticism. Terrorists blowing themselves up in a bus full of people. Christians going on crusades. Jews isolating themselves from the rest of society ..."

I knew she was referring to the Hasidic Jews, but decided not to correct her.

"The Amish," she said adding to her list. "Or religious people living in a commune in the jungle somewhere and then killing themselves because the leader tells them to. Crazy crap like that."

The more examples she offered, the more intense she got, leaning toward me as she spoke, her volume going up a notch or two.

"Oh," I said. "That kind of crazy crap."

Frowning, she leaned back in her chair. "Sorry," she said. "I didn't mean to get so ..."

"Fanatical?"

"Ha, ha," she said. "You know what I mean."

Emily was average looking, but she was not average. She was smart and passionate. She just didn't understand the nature of what she was complaining about.

"Yes," I said. "I know what you mean. And I think what you are meaning to ask is, what's going on inside a person's head when they act in a way that, to some people, seems irrational?"

"Yeah, sure. I guess."

"It's not really a religious question, it is a psychological question."

"How come you only see it in religious people?"

"You don't see it only in religious people. You see it in all kinds of people who are intensely committed to an idea or a goal, whether the idea is perceived by others as bad or good."

She considered me for a moment and drank some of her coffee. "Can you give me some examples?" she said finally.

"Olympic athletes who get up every morning at five o'clock and train hours every day for years to compete in the Olympics."

"That's not the same. They're not killing anyone."

"Neither are the Amish or the Hasidic Jews that you mentioned."

She was mildly put off that I wasn't going to let her get away with anything.

"That's only one example," she said, "but I expect that you could probably come up with others. Conner said you were really smart. Use to be a professor, and now you work for some think tank and write books."

"Well, I don't know about being really smart, but he's right about the other two."

"So you come here every day," Emily said, "and talk to people about stuff?"

"I don't talk to people every day, but most."

"How come?"

"I like it. Since I'm not in the classroom anymore, I miss the interaction with people. Writing is a lonely profession. This gives me a chance to interact with young people."

As she drank some of her coffee, she looked like she was trying to decide whether or not she liked me.

I don't know what she decided, but she said, "So what is the psychology of fanaticism?"

"Good question," I said. "You're pretty smart yourself. Some people think fanaticism is a disease, like alcoholism. It isn't. They only say that because they are not deeply passionate about anything. The kind of behavior that is sometimes considered fanatical is the product of a certain kind of personality, which is probably the result of a certain kind of an environmental situation. For instance, let's use your example of religious fanaticism as it relates to Islam. First, not all Muslims are fanatics regarding their religion. Some, depending on where and how they were raised and how educated they are, are quite fanatical. Muslims who live in Muslim communities and receive only a strict Muslim education, which consists of reading only the Quran, appear to be the most fanatical."

"So you're saying it is a matter of education," she said.

"That's one component, I believe. There are others," I said. "Did you ever know a person who, no matter what the subject was, always seemed to take an extreme position or react to an idea in an extreme way?"

140

She thought for a moment. "Yeah. Went to high school with a girl like that."

"Some people seem to have what might be called a reactionary personality. Doesn't matter what the situation is, they always seem to over react or react in an extreme manner. Some think it might be associated with low self-esteem, or an overly developed sense of right and wrong, the need to be right all the time—which ties back in to low self-esteem. There are a number of explanations as to why people develop a reactionary personality. Those kinds of people sometimes tend to become fanatical about some things."

"Okay, but is that the case with something like wanting to be an Olympic champion?"

"No. I think usually in those cases the person is driven by a desire to be the best. A businessperson can be another example. Works all the time and often sacrifices everything else to become a success. Some people call them a workaholic. They are driven by a singular focus to accomplish a singular goal."

"And you think that's the same thing as religious fanaticism?"

"No. It's not the same. It's similar. It generates a similar kind of singular focus and commitment."

"Do you think it's a good thing?"

"I think any kind of extreme behavior can be harmful. Ultimately, I think it has to do with the goal to which one is committed."

"You think the goal of killing people that disagree with you is a good goal?"

"Of course not."

"But a lot of religious fanatics," Emily said, "want to kill people who disagree with them."

"That's true. And that's a bad thing. And sometimes they are so committed to their beliefs that the only way to respond to a person like that is to kill them before they kill you."

Her eyebrows went up and she leaned back slightly as if my words carried a physical force that impacted her. "It's surprising that you would say that."

"Why?"

"Well, you're a Christian. Connor says you used to be a minister."

"That's right."

"Aren't most ministers pacifists?"

"No. Most of us have had enough dealings with evil to know that sometimes the only way to defeat it is to destroy it."

"Geez, what does that mean?"

"The eternal struggle between good and evil. In the end, for one to triumph, the other one will have to be destroyed."

"You're talking about the Bible now, aren't you. Satan and Jesus and all that?"

"Yes. Sounds kind of fanatical, doesn't it?"

"Are you a fanatic?"

"I don't think so. But let me ask you, have you ever felt so completely dedicated to something that you would willingly die for it?"

"No."

"That's why fanaticism is so confusing to you."

"What's that supposed to mean?"

"You have no personal frame of reference for understanding someone feeling so committed to something that they would die for it."

"Or kill for it?" she said aggressively. "You bet I don't. Do you?"

"Not in the sense you mean it."

"What other sense is there?"

"Emily, you need to calm down. I'm not the enemy. I'm trying to help you understand something that you have never experienced."

She was frowning, not happy with what I was saying.

"There are some fanatics who do horrible things in the name of whatever it is they believe. We all know that, and people who do not share their beliefs condemn their behavior. I think you and I agree on that. But to call all people who have strong religious beliefs fanatics is to put them in the category with people who commit mass murder in the name of religion. And that is simply not right. And to say that people who have strong religious beliefs have a disease, like alcoholism, is also wrong. What I'd like to help you understand is that people can have very strong feelings about any number of things, and be deeply committed to those things, without hurting themselves or other people."

"But isn't telling other people that their religion is wrong, and that they must believe as you believe, hurtful?"

"Why would that be hurtful? Lots of people feel that the sports team they like is the best team, and that other teams are not as good. Lots of people believe their brand of car or truck they buy is the best on the road and that other brands are not as good. I've heard people say that the kind of car I drive sucks because it is not the kind they drive. I've heard people say that the football team I like sucks because it is not the team they like. Is that hurtful?"

Emily didn't say anything. I did not feel the need to push her for a response, so I said, "If you can tell people their car or their sports team isn't as good as yours, why can't you tell them their religion isn't as good as yours?"

"It just doesn't seem right. That's why."

"From your perspective," I said.

"From everyone's perspective."

"No, that's not right. Only some people believe that religious zeal is unacceptable. And those people are usually not religious people and have no idea what it means to believe deeply in a given set of religious beliefs."

"So, you're saying that unless someone is religious, they can't understand religious beliefs?"

"That's what I'm saying."

She didn't have a response ready, so I kept going.

"Do you think Connor or I can really understand what it's like to be a woman? Understand all the concerns, the pressures, the anxieties, the needs?"

She laughed. "No."

"Do you think you can really understand what it is like to be a man?"

"Men are not all that hard to understand."

"Answer the question. Do you think you really understand what it's like to be a man, to understand the pressures we feel, our worries, our insecurities, our drives to succeed, to be the kind of a man that a woman would want to be with? To measure up to other men? To our own standards of manhood? You think you can understand that?"

Grudgingly she said, "No."

"Then how can a person who is not deeply religious understand what that means to be deeply religious?"

"I don't know," she admitted. "Maybe you're right."

Ah. Progress.

She thought for a moment as she sipped her coffee. "Okay, say you're right about some religious people. They are deeply religious, and so they are kind of fanatical about some things, but they're not hurting anyone. Maybe calling them fanatics is not accurate. But some people are fanatical about their beliefs. What about them?"

"There are some people who kill in the name of religion. They do not represent all religious people. Throughout history there have been people who were not religious and killed tens of millions of people in the name of some other cause. Hitler killed many millions of people in the name of conquest and power. Had nothing to do with religious beliefs. The socialist leaders of the 20th century killed over 100 million people in China and the Soviet Union in the name of socialism. Had nothing to do with religious beliefs."

"Okay, so there is more than one kind of fanaticism. That doesn't make religious fanaticism acceptable."

"Any form of zealous fanaticism," I said, "that causes pain and suffering is evil and needs to be stopped."

"But you are saying that being deeply religious doesn't make you a fanatic that hurts people."

"Yes."

"Okay, I see that. But what makes some people hurt other people in the name of religion. I mean religion is supposed to be about goodness and kindness and helping people and all that. Why would someone use religion as an excuse to hurt people?"

"I think that some of it has to do with the religion some people embrace. I think some of it has to do with a misunderstanding of their religion."

"Can you give me an example?"

"Sure. The Crusades of the Middle Ages provide a perfect example. The Europeans who called themselves Christians were Christians in name only. Many of them couldn't even read. Of those who could read, most never read the Bible. They did not even begin to understand what real Christianity was. They were sincere and zealous. But they were utterly misguided. So, they behaved in a way that God was not happy with. What they did was wrong."

"Could you say the same thing about Islamic fundamentalism?" Emily asked.

"I believe so. There are many Muslims who do not agree with their more fundamentalist brothers in the faith. They prefer to be peaceful and allow people of other faiths to believe and practice their faith even though they believe them to be mistaken in their beliefs. Many Christians feel the same way. They believe Muslims are mistaken, but they do not believe God wants them to kill people who are not Christians."

"So some religious people are just confused."

"Because they have been misled," I said.

"But their being taught something that is not true," Emily said, "and their acting on what they were taught, doesn't make religion a bad thing, it makes the people who misled them and the people who allowed themselves to be misled bad people."

I said, "Basically, yes. But I would add that expecting people who have been taught something from childhood to engage in serious analysis of what they were taught to determine whether or not it is correct is something most people are not equipped to do on their own."

"So you're saying they are not responsible for the evil things they do in the name of their religion?"

"No, I'm not saying they are not responsible. I think most people who have a normal level of intelligence can figure out that killing non-combatants simply because they do not believe what you believe is not a good thing to do, regardless of what you have been taught. I think most Western people have a very strong orientation toward justice, and believe that individuals are accountable for their actions. But I also believe that if you have been taught something from childhood, in a closed community where no one has ever questioned what is being taught, that beginning to question it, though not impossible, is not easy. And not everyone does it. Many simply do as they have been taught. And because of that, people suffer and die. God cannot be happy with that."

"So, you're saying that religious fanaticism is not God's fault."

"Definitely not God's fault."

"But if different religions are different ways of worshiping God, why doesn't God see to it that those different religions get it right instead of getting it wrong?"

"Because human beings are self-determined. They make choices about what they believe and what they do or don't do."

"But isn't God supposed to be in charge of everything?"

"God is sovereign. But in his sovereignty he decided to create humans in his image, that is, to make them the same kind of thinking beings that he is. Since humans are rational beings, they are also, necessarily, free to choose. Being rational and being self-determined are different sides of the same coin."

"So, God's not in control of everything."

"No, he's not. You cannot control self-determined beings. They are self-controlled. There's lots of stuff that happens in the world that God is not happy with. A lot of it is done in the name of religion. Because the people doing evil claim to be doing it in the name of God does not mean that God has anything to do with it."

"Okay," Emily said. "So you can't really hold God or religious people in general accountable for evil that some do in the name of religion. But does religion actually do anything good or helpful in the world?"

"Sure. All kinds of good stuff."

"Like what?"

"There are over 400,000 full-time Christian missionaries serving around the world in various capacities, all of them doing good things, making a difference in the world."

"What kind of things?"

"Teaching in schools, running orphanages, serving as medical missionaries, digging wells to provide clean water, training people in different trades so they can earn a living. Lives are being saved; lives are being changed. Lots of good being is done by religious people who give up comfortable lives here at home to go live in a less comfortable situation. In fact, I'd be willing to bet that there is much more good being done by religious people than bad being done by religious people."

"How come you don't hear about all the good being done?"

"Because the news media, which is made up of mostly non-religious people, would rather focus on the bad so they can make religion look like a force for bad in the world."

"That's a pretty cynical explanation."

"Nope. It's just the truth. People who have rejected religion don't like religion or religious people."

"Why not?"

"Because many of the things the non-religious approve of and participate in, religion, especially Christianity, condemns. And they don't like being told that they are doing wrong, and that if they do not stop, God will punish them."

"So they want to make religion look like a bad thing instead of a good thing?"

"Yes."

"Can you prove that?"

"All you have to do is read the reports from Christian missionaries and all that is being done in the world. When you see how much good is being done and not reported by any media outlet, all you have to do is ask why. If they were interested in reporting good news, they would. They are not, so they don't. Why not? Because they don't want people to see how much good religious people do around the world. If something bad happens, which it does occasionally because there are no perfect people, the news reports that. But all the good that is done goes unreported."

"I didn't know any of this."

"I know."

"You've been very patient with me," Emily said. "I appreciate that. You helped me understand."

"I'm glad I was able to help."

"And you've made me want to learn more."

I smiled. "I'm glad."

"Can I come back and talk to you again?"

"Absolutely."

Conclusion

The characters in this small book have asked a lot of questions. Dr. Baker has answered them. Some of his answers were factual; some were his opinion. You may agree with what Dr. Baker says, or you may not. The important thing is that you consider the questions, think about the answers, and decide whether you agree or not. For some of the questions, you may not yet be sure whether you agree or not. That is understandable. The thing to do in that case is to continue to think about them until you form an opinion. And even then, you need to continue to think about them. Talk about them with other thoughtful people. The dialectic process will be helpful. It is my sincere hope that reading this material has been both interesting and helpful to you.

www.ingramcontent.com/pod-product-compliance
Lightning Source LLC
LaVergne TN
LVHW011202080426
835508LV00007B/548